My Waterloo

Stories

Paul Bland

PAUL BLAND

Elm Leaf Publishing
New York, NY

1

ISBN:978-0999603529
Published by Elm Leaf Publishing
New York, NY

Printed in the United States of America

To my Iowa family
and friends.

Prologue

That day in late October or early November is gone. A fall day when I am looking out of a window at my junior high school and at the bare trees and leaf-covered ground. The magic of fall is fading. And the colder weather will force us to wear warmer clothing and coats. In this classroom, we are told stories and we read poems. And I think about the meaning of the words being spoken; never really grasping their full force.

My Waterloo, Iowa is a place made of memories. It is American in its character. American being Midwestern, simple and influenced by the cultural and social shifts we have all experienced over the past few decades as Americans. The changing seasons are the most memorable part of this setting. As I grew up into adulthood, my perspective of them changed but they remained as elements tied to the land and sky. And to my childhood perception of the world. A doorway to my own imagination. I love describing them in my writing as I am always amazed by their beauty and their larger spiritual meaning. If I have a poetic side, they are at the heart of it.

In this book I describe the most ordinary things. But it is the culmination of these small facts and events that make up the days, months and years I have experienced here. Most of it is gone. Like a hat gone out of style. A photograph tinted with the color of another bygone era. One you wish to remember, if for only a moment.

My most recent visit home was this past year during a Christmas holiday. It seemed as if the Waterloo, Iowa I remember is only seen in remnants. And yet, with the Christmas decorations in the yards and with the snowy Iowa weather, a bit of magic was still in the air. The fact that I had made the effort to come home had made the difference.

Chapter 1

_____

Waterloo, Iowa 2002

It was a winter's morning. The Cedar River in downtown Waterloo and the trees along its banks were covered in ice and snow. The sun was glowing behind a cloud-covered, gray sky. It was a morning for going to work, for a breakfast of coffee, eggs and toast. It was a time for school and for rising, because you were alive and able to face the bitter cold.

That day reminded me of the winter months I had experienced in Iowa as a child and as an adolescent. The memory of it seemed far away. I belonged here and yet, I did not, having outgrown a reason. I did have family here and it was my hometown. I had returned here from New York City. I had decided to go home. This was home, this small town in Northeastern Iowa.

A December month, 1960s

Joy is sometimes mixed with the ordinary, the start of it in your heart and it was like this for us one snowy morning in December. It was already the twenty-first of the month and it was snowing just as predicted. My mother and I were downtown and having parked our car, a boxy beige _Ford_, we were about to do our first and only Christmas shopping. Every year as I could remember, the same Christmas decorations re-appeared along with the gray Iowa winter sky. Attached to the downtown street-light posts were S-shapes in red and silver garland. S e a s o n 's G r e e t i n g s spelled out in tin foil and lights, danced above East 4th Street with each gust of a chilling, winter wind.

As a young boy, I looked forward to Christmas with growing excitement and yet, I had grown more ambivalent about this holiday. I was acutely aware of its religious significance, my father's somewhat reluctant participation and my mother's efforts despite a lack of money. My mother was a petite, pretty lady with reddish-brown hair and hazel eyes, energetic and strong-willed but at times she was a bit, well, self-deprecating. Even as a child I was aware of her small fears and self-doubts. Today she wore a nice dress, warm wool coat and gloves. I was wearing a blue jacket and a stocking cap.

The streets of our downtown area were busy with activity and a thin, fresh blanket of white snow now covered the streets and sidewalks. The perfect setting for our Christmas errands. I made note of everything as we walked. The Chinese restaurant with its dragon wallpaper, glowing white lanterns and now strings of Christmas twinkle lights decorated one mirrored wall. The people inside the restaurant were eating and talking, their packages propped up next to them in the red vinyl booths. We continued walking, past the Jeweler's window display of shiny, polished silver and then into *Black's Department Store. Black's* was the most elegant store in town, built around 1914-1920. The first-floor lobby had a very high ceiling and fluted interior columns. In the center of the store and displayed above the merchandise counters was now a row of perfectly shaped Christmas trees with colored lights. On top of the glass and metal counters were red and green satin ornaments in artificial pine-boughs. If you looked up, you would see an open mezzanine level flanked with oak arm chairs reserved for elderly, white-haired souls starring down at the first-floor activity as if in retail heaven.

We stopped at one of the counters to purchase chocolates by the pound and my mother's voice took on the same pleasant tone of the sales clerk's as she counted out the money and requested that the box be wrapped.

"I'd like that wrapped please. Oh my, isn't that pretty!" she said, noticing the gold wrapping on a box of chocolates tied with a plaid ribbon; the script on the box like a fancy glint of some larger urban place.

Our candy too was covered in gold paper and then placed in a crisp, gray *Black's* paper bag. Other purchases were made that afternoon including a green velvet fabric for my sister's Christmas dress and a gift for my brother, but with the streetlights illuminating brighter in the fading afternoon light and falling snow, it was time to pick up my father from work. We stopped once more to admire a dime store window display of glittering boxed ornaments and heated bubbling light sets, before heading back to the car and an expired parking meter.

This was a factory town. Most men worked at either the tractor factory or the meat packing plant. My dad worked at the meat packing plant. Soon we found ourselves waiting in front of the plant and my father finally appeared in a line of other men walking through a metal gateway. My mother moved over to the passenger side as he approached the car and I was warned not to mention our extravagant purchases. There was always a silence in the car as we drove away from the tall brick building and the foul, stinking smell of the slaughterhouse that faded with the beginnings of conversation.

That evening my father brought in a tree, a nice-smelling spruce but much too thin to my liking. I was told to retrieve our decorations from the attic closet. This an odd assortment of ornaments, light-sets and an unreliable red metal star with a single, blinking bulb. The tree belonged in the woods it told us silently, but once decorated it would be more than adequate, I told myself. I personally attended to forgotten details such as the placement of the nativity on the piano and taping up lights around our front window. Then several trips were made outside to view the results, half a tree visible, framed in twinkle lights and a stubborn, dark star shape on top. I had repaired the twinkle lights that now framed the window with black electrician's tape and aluminum foil. A miracle my mother had declared. This had taken some effort and yet, unbelievably they still flickered occasionally. Christmas Eve was in my mother's voice and found in boxes of cookies frosted green. What were those tiny silver candies that decorated each sugar and flour cookie? Christmas morning arrived and after opening my gifts, I took careful inventory, and arranged the items in a box. There was Christmas dinner to prepare and my father always managed to find some incidental chore even on Christmas morning.

Christmas 1980s

Two decades had passed since that December month and as I had done many times before, I was returning home at Christmas time from New York City to Iowa by *Amtrak* train. l had made my usual connection in Chicago, Illinois. I had waited for hours with the other holiday travelers in the comfortable but noisy *Amtrak* lounge at Union Station in Chicago. The passenger waiting area and lounge was decorated with a flocked Christmas tree and metallic looking, cardboard chiming bells.

I was now on a train that would take me as far as Dubuque, Iowa. The train had been late in leaving that morning. I loved the gleam of the trains, the echoes of sounds on the train platform. I looked out from the train at the vast rail yards as the train slowly pulled out from Union Station. It was frigid outside, and the railway workmen's breath hung in the air. In shadow or sunlight these lonely rail yards were an unchanging part of the big rural city. In the distance was the towering skyline of Chicago.

The day had warmed with the sound of the faster moving train. The town of Chicago an early morning memory. From my window, I could now see the length of the train as it moved slowly across the bridge that connected Illinois and Iowa; the dark vastness of the

10

Mississippi river below. We had just crept past the brown-gray, wooded marshland that edged the wide river. I stared out at the buildings on the Iowa side of the river where my parents waited. I had not been home for many years and that dark expanse of the Mississippi seemed symbolic of the geographic and emotional distance between us. The *Amtrak* train would take me as far as Dubuque and they were to drive me the rest of the way home to Waterloo.

Finally, after starts and stops, there was the sound of the train's final grinding halt and I left my train seat, feeling tired and a bit apprehensive. There the two stood in view, in the cold of midday. I saw my father first, he was wearing glasses now, his hair grayer and a bit heavier. My mother had changed the most and the usual brightness in her eyes had dimmed.

"I hardly recognized you!" said mother, with great joy at seeing me. Dad smiled politely. They had dressed up for the occasion.

We conversed in the car with an awkward formality that faded to quiet happiness as we made the drive home past flat, snow-covered fields and a gray afternoon sky.

Our small house had acquired modest changes and my mother proudly pointed these out to me; a shelf to display plates, a clock with chimes, paint and new curtains. Careful attention had been paid to the Christmas tree, a long-needle evergreen full and squat. Our assortment of ornaments had expanded as a result of after-Christmas bargains not resisted. Across the street from our house, strings of

Christmas lights outlined a row of newly-built rectangular houses.

It seemed that the *Rath* meat-packing plant where my father had worked for three decades had finally closed after many unprofitable years and he now looked-for work where it might be found. He had not adjusted well my mother had confided to me. The part-time work and yard jobs he had found did not fill his days. I felt relief for him for he had escaped the ugly, unhealthy place alive. But he had been proud of being useful, of being hard-working and that had been taken away from him. It was the worst thing you could take from a man. His work and with it his identity. It was in the past and now unattainable like his former youth. It must have shadowed everything he did, and his manner showed it. He now shared the house but didn't really own it. But he seemed to appreciate my mother more and that was nice to see. I liked him for this and for many other things. He always kept busy and worked hard. He was creative and artistic in small ways. A "man's man" my mother would say.

The new shopping mall of stores had opened on the Southwest edge of town along with a new *K-Mart* and new grocery supermarkets on the way, but my mother expressed no interest in going there and with a prescription needing to be filled, we headed downtown to *Osco Drug*.

At this point, most of the downtown retail stores had been vacated but the same S-shaped, tinsel-garland street lamp decorations were up. They sparkled in the afternoon sunlight. The sunlight casting long shadows from the corners of the empty buildings. As we walked back to the car my mother stopped, stopped as if stopping time itself, and expressed her happiness at my being home. I said very little and seeing a glimmer of sadness on her face, I suddenly felt my own. I was to return to New York City in a few days and although she had my father to keep her company she would in a sense, be alone. We were alike in many ways. We had shared secrets on holidays. We had laughed together at inappropriate times. She had always been my best friend.

That evening I went outside. And I stood looking at our front picture window to get a view of our tree framed in twinkle lights. It was snowing. A light, silent snow that forgave all bad memories of the place. I walked a distance; looked towards the Brown's sleepy house on the opposite corner of our street. Moonlight illuminated the snow-covered ground and had turned it a pale blue. A light more a part of the cold of snow itself and separate from the warm reflected incandescent light from the windows of the houses cast on the snow as well. I then walked a few blocks from our house. Our neighborhood as magical as the singular sound of crunching snow under my feet. I reached the corner lot where the *Lion's Club* sold Christmas trees each year. Leftover trees remained in the lot, bundled and green. The string of light bulbs hung from the shed to lot fence dark. In the distance behind the houses were the tops of taller trees, trees apart of the wooded area that edged this neighborhood; a gray-brown haze of branches.

For whatever the reason, life circumstances, a lack of money or my own impatience as a young man, I would be home for only a few days and the time passed quickly. Christmas morning arrived, silly and early and after the gifts had been opened, my father and I sat in the living room and talked. My mother happily adding to our sparse conversation from the kitchen. My father got up to look for a photo album. I then sat under the tree and with legs crossed and as I had done as a kid, I carefully arranged my gifts in a box. This time not taking inventory.

Chapter 2

The rain brought out yellow raincoats and galoshes. The headlights and swooshing windshield wipers on cars. It made the streets wet and reflective. Looking out at the rain from the front picture window of our house, I could see rain water flooding the water drain in the center of our yard near the street. It would have been an unremarkable thing to witness, if I had not been a child. But it was the most dramatic thing I had ever seen. The sky was a dark gray. There was the lightening, silence and then crashing, booming thunder. The water around the drain now threatened our yard and completely covered sections of the sidewalk. It ran down the sides of our tar street in torrents.

It rained a lot during the 1960s in our small town of Waterloo, Iowa. A record rainfall that also flooded the *Black Hawk Creek* area not far from our house. When the rain had stopped to a dripping from trees, the sun would reappear. An edge of it at first from behind the gray clouds. The tall, scraggly pine tree in our neighbor's yard was wet with raindrops now catching the sunlight. A rainbow might appear in the sky as well. That arc of brilliant colors that never looked quite real. Worms appeared in the mud-covered sidewalk and countless leaves floated down the water drain along with the rain water. The grass in the yard was soaked. The sun would warm us again. The April rain a memory.

Our house was on the West side of town and on Summit Street. It was a small house built in the 1930s, with wood floors and a tiny foyer that led into a living room. The rest of the house included two very small bedrooms, a kitchen and a dining area, a basement and an attic. My father would add an addition to this house during the 1960s. I remember the excitement surrounding this event. The workman's pencil notes on the unfinished kitchen cupboards, the smell of chalky sheet-rock and the Danish-modern dining room set bought new. A new garage was built and its size dwarfed our small house. The front yard was close to the sidewalk and the backyard was adequate with an Elm tree and a lilac bush. Peonies, orange lilies and rhubarb grew along one side of a fence that divided our yard from our neighbors. On a warm afternoon laundry waved on our drooping clothesline. The backyard was an entryway to the vacant field behind our house. The yard mowed or the grass overgrown and with dandelions and scattered violets. On warm summer days, I would sit near the flowers and rhubarb that grew alongside the fence. There were blackberries ripe and sweet on a blackberry bush.

It is another summer in Waterloo, Iowa. Along the fence in our backyard, there are blooming and shriveling orange lilies and peonies in different shades of pink. I walk to the *Reber Avenue Corner Grocery* store for lunch meat and American cheese for sandwiches on white bread with too much mayonnaise. There is lemonade frozen from a can and served in *Tupperware* plastic glasses of pastel colors. It might be sunny out or overcast and too humid. A rainstorm might bring us indoors and then we remember the past; days of rain from earlier summers and seasons

How could a lilac tree be of any real importance? Imagine the approach of a summer, a dry humid hot summer with nothing to do. The lilac tree has bloomed in our back yard. It is still cool in the afternoon. In the morning, the grass is wet with cold dew against bare feet. The lilac tree in our backyard represented spring, warmer weather and then the quick passing of time. The blooms were soon gone. Some had been on our dining room table in a green-glass vase. But most of them had dried on the branch, their fragrance dying as well, shriveling from violet to brown. You couldn't bring them back. It was the same when losing a person, a friend for whatever reason. It was a part of life. But you grew more appreciative of the past, of what you had been offered. And we had our lilac tree.

This old couple used to come to visit my mother. They were old-fashioned in their manner and dress. They were more a part of things spiritual; not worldly.

"We just thought we would take a little trip today. We brought you some rhubarb from the garden."

This old couple people lived out on Airline Highway in a farmhouse still standing. They had a large vegetable and flower garden. I knew this because we had visited their place. The furniture in their house was old and made of dark mahogany and oak. There

17

were pieces of porcelain and pottery in a glass-door cabinet. Green house plants flourished near the sunny windows. The rhubarb they had brought looked gigantic compared to the narrow stalks of it that grew in our back yard.

"Oh, why thank you. That's very sweet of you. I 'll make a pie with those," said mother.

About this time, I wrote a poem that made it in the *Whittier Grade School* literary compilation. This was a haiku poem about a grasshopper, grass and dew, singing a water song. There it was in bright blue ink for the world to see! Raindrops are falling, In the grass the grasshopper, Sings a water song.

It is an evening in March. Our parents have been invited to our elementary school to see our work and meet our homeroom teacher. The Tuesday evening arrives. I approach the schoolhouse with my parents. The lights are all on in the two-story brick schoolhouse. The big windows a view into the schoolrooms with their pastel-painted glossy walls and blackboards. My school work has been carefully placed on my desk. The alphabet script I had practiced so carefully is one of the pages. It has a gold star on it. The milk-glass light fixtures hanging from the ceiling glow against the dark of night seen through the large windows of the class room. My homeroom teacher, who always looks very nice, looks even better tonight. She is more dressed up and wears a corsage of pink and white carnations given to her by our principle. She meets mom and dad and seems more distant with me, but she is always smiling.

"Paul is a very good student." And then she moves on to the next introduction of parents.

Each night in my bedroom I polished the pair of black, buckled shoes that I wore to school using *Johnson's* liquid shoe polish that stained my hands. I made paper and paste collages from colorful magazine pages for my weekly third-grade project at grade school. A collage that told a story. I always got an E for excellent.

Sunday morning and often Sunday evening was a time when we went to our Wesleyan church. I wore a white shirt, a good pair of slacks and sometimes a sports jacket bought at *Sears Roebuck* or *JC Penny*. One of these sports jackets was a gold and green plaid. Wednesday evening could also be a night for church attendance if there was a special service to attend or if one of my parents announced that we should go like good Christians do. Traveling preachers and their wives who sang or played the piano would visit. Or missionaries returning from a foreign land showed films of island villages or mountainous regions where uneducated peoples had not heard about the lord. These Wednesday church services always seemed more tied to the darkness of night. It was mid-week and people went to work the next day. The congregation was much smaller and we sat near the front of the sanctuary. Holidays such as Halloween or the Fourth of July were tied to church as well, for we would witness the evidence of these celebrations going to or returning from church. Passing through the neighborhoods on our way home. There was something about church services that made us

19

more respectable. We were to be good, to have faith in Christ the lord. And so, we were less conscious of the fact that we were poor. But not so poor that we ever relied on charity as my parents never accepted this or used credit to make a purchase.

My father worked at *Rath* and my mother was a housewife. When she did work it was doing house work for others who needed a lady to help with this sort of thing. Much later in life, she would return to school, go to Hawkeye Community College and earn an undergraduate degree in marketing.

We were so proud of her for this accomplishment.

It is an evening in October. The night air is chilly and it is certain that fall has commenced toward winter. Summer is over and the yards have more leaves at their edges clinging to bushes and fences, scattered on the grass still green.

It is a cold fall day in November, so cold that it foretells winter. The wind blows piles of leaves into the air. A coat is needed. The branches of trees sway against a gray sky. Halloween has passed and thanksgiving will be celebrated within the month. Only sparrows are seen. The fallen, dry leaves rustle in the wind.

It is winter in Iowa. Looking outdoors, there are drifts of snow several feet high. The windows of the house rattle in the winter wind. Ice and snow cling to the brown shingles and roof of the old house next door. The field behind our house is covered with a blanket of snow. There are rabbits seen in winter or the flash of a pheasant, an

20

occasional red cardinal; sparrows and crows. The January month comes cold and silent. It is the month of my birthday. The weather cold and severe and yet my birthday important; celebrated with a cake, cards and gifts all the same.

The deep winter snow seemed pitiless. The dried, brown weeds rags in its drifts. The wind blew the snow into swirls of crystal ice particles. Winter days in Iowa were sometimes bright with sunshine or as dark as early nightfall. It weathered wood and made it wet in spring. Finally melting to reveal the brown earth of spring. It was tied to memories of bitter cold mornings and billowy exhaust rising from chimneys and cars. As you grew older it simply flanked a shoveled sidewalk, but it was always partially magic, swirling and sparkling and lonely; only seen by yourself.

The winter wind howls outside. I look out the window at our neighbor's tar-shingled, two-story house. A light is on in the kitchen. Snowdrifts cover the ground around the old house and attached woodshed. The bushes behind the house have snow caught in their branches. In spring, these same bushes will bloom tiny white blossoms, not unlike the clumps of snow that now cover them. It is day for trekking outside.

In the spring, we would go to the *Rainbow Greenhouse* to buy plants for the yard. We would pass by this abandoned, tall factory building on the way to the greenhouse. Past the dusty, broken windows of the towering, empty factory and then onto the freshness of living greenhouse plants.

The plants with flowers had been carefully placed in table sections creating a force of blooms of the same color; pink, red, purple or orange. Flowers like petunias, miniature marigolds, geraniums; familiar flower-bed fillers for sun or shade. There were bunches of pink, red and white carnations and roses in refrigerated cases for special occasions. Then it was back to a gravel road and past the grass-covered fields that surrounded this more remote part of town.

There was a couple that lived next-door to us. They were young, almost newlyweds and with one young son. They had a modern, split-level house with a flat roof and they drank beer. They had a motorboat parked in their driveway. The young woman wore stretch slacks and her husband tinkered with things in the garage. They were a TV sitcom. They probably even bowled. Bowling alleys were for those people who lived differently than us. They bought impractical things they didn't need and worse, were big drinkers and never went to church. They painted their flat-roofed house a dark chocolate brown and in the spring the Cherry tree in their backyard would bloom into a mass of pink blossoms, some reaching our yard. Their pine tree edged our yard. a tall pine tree with sky spaces between its branches. With small curly pinecones, fragrant evergreen needles and peeling, gray bark revealing an orange-gold color. No one noticed the tree or trees, but me it seemed.

There was another couple on the corner of our block that also lived in a mid-century style house with a flat roof. This was a much smaller house than the flat-roofed house next door to us. The couple on the corner had two adorable children, a pretty girl and a handsome boy, both with dark hair and eyes. The mother was slim and pretty. It was rumored that she was addicted to *Pepsi-Cola*. I had been inside this house as well. In the living room, a color television set would be tuned to a game show and commercials. There was a tall counter and bar stools visible from the living room. A big bowl of potato chips was always on the counter and next to this were -bottles of *Pepsi*.

On Saturday evenings, my father made us popcorn with apple slices. This was before *Jiffy Pop* or popcorn makers. We would watch television. What else was there to do on a Saturday night? In the summer, he made us homemade ice cream with too much vanilla flavoring. I remember our endless cranking of the ice cream maker as ice spilt out from the top. *Morton Salt* was poured onto the ice to melt it faster. As a young teenager, frozen pizza was affordable and was often consumed with *Pepsi* or *Coke* at church youth group meetings. Or while watching a late-night, horror movie with my reliable friend up the street on his parents old, floor-model TV set. I loved the crunchiness of the pizza crust, the canned tomato sauce and the almost tasteless cheese on top. It was just as good as the photo of it on the waxy pizza box.

My brother owned a pair of bongo drums about this time. I mention these things because they are what defined us, being middle class, typically Midwestern and greatly influenced by television.

Television was our window to the world. A glass tube enclosed in a light-cherry, varnished wood box and with a speaker covered in a nubby fabric. The box had legs. *Zenith* was the brand name on it; purchased at the appliance store downtown. Images of NASA space launches appeared before us. National news events with the setting of far-away places. Familiar characters we knew in sitcoms faced weekly dilemmas, as canned laughter responded to the silly storylines.

The local television channel was KWWL. There was a local news program and advertisements for area businesses. This local station sometimes interrupted our usual programs to deliver weather bulletins; tornado warnings and snow storms, or likely flooding. When it went silent, we were left to our usual surroundings. The front and back yard. The street we lived on. The local grocery store and the changing weather. The sky became our courier of news. The hourly position of the sun if seen, and the elements of the season that altered our mood.

The downtown area of Waterloo, Iowa that was on the West side of the Cedar River, had a sporting-goods shop and a hobby shop that sold balsa-wood airplanes, model cars, glues, kites and train-sets. There was at one time, a place that sold used books and copies of comics. There was a *Woolworth's* dime store, an appliance store, a *JC Penny* and a *Montgomery Ward's*. There have always been several bars. On the East side of downtown, a buffet-style restaurant was popular named *Bishops*. A charming lady with bouffant, bleach-blond hair was the hostess there for years and years. The food was good and this place relocated to the two shopping center malls, but they are now closed. High-school age kids worked behind the food counters. During this time, a ride on the local bus was .25. It took you past the pleasant, tree-shaded houses on Third Street, then past *Byrnes Park* golf course and then downtown. The *Grout Museum* was free then. There were displays of arrow heads, gem stones, cabin interiors with wax pioneers, a small planetarium with a cardboard cutout of Waterloo's skyline. Nighttime in Iowa was crickets and the smell of mowed grass, the sound of gravel heard through a screen door, a TV set on somewhere. The corner grocery closed for the day.

The *Woolworth's* downtown had a lunch counter. There was an *A & W* root beer stand out near Evansdale. Evansdale is one of those small towns that edges Waterloo. There's a lumber yard there as well. Anyway, nothing extraordinary except that the *A & W* was out in a more rural area, on a highway really, lit up at night with fluorescent lighting. That was part of the magic of the place. There was a bakery on West 5th Street; *Johnson's Bakery*. This bakery was where you could get a white sheet-cake with special messages and decoration frosting for events like school graduations, showers, weddings or relatives visiting. Sample birthday and wedding cakes were displayed in its window.

We bought most of our groceries at *Eagle's* grocery store. It had an arched ceiling with a neon eagle on its façade. It was a larger grocery, perhaps the largest in Waterloo at that time. *Eagle's* grocery was air-cooled in the summer months, the vegetables and fruit on slanted displays were water-sprayed by a timer device and there was an intercom voice system that echoed against the arched, metal ceiling. We bought what we needed, mostly. On its shelves were *Aunt Jemima* pancake flour and syrup, *Betty Crocker* cake mixes, boxed breakfast cereal, *Campbell's Soup* (Tomato a favorite), 5 lb. bags of potatoes, carrots, cartons of eggs, hamburger meat, chicken and pot roast and *Archer Farms* cookies. There were those small, square cookies that looked like patent-leather shoes that were filled with marsh-mellow and a graham-cracker crust. I loved those cookies. This was a place frequented so often that it was tied to the weather, a growing rain storm, stifling summer heat and humidity or a blizzard snowfall. *Eagle's* grocery was a place where you might stop off quickly to get one half dozen eggs for a cake and run into someone from church or a neighbor. It wasn't that you didn't want to see them, but you didn't look your best and you were in a hurry. But that was usually the least of your worries. Relatives from Des Moines were coming. The cake wasn't baked. The house was a mess.

When I was young, I used to go with a parent to *Osco Drugstore* downtown on the East side. It was usually for something that was needed but nothing more. In the aisles of this store were things for sale such as lawn sprinklers and seasonal items. Plastic beach balls for the non-existent pool or seaside resort. Container rock gardens that grew exotic plants that didn't look real. Halloween costumes and masks that we would not buy because of the cost.

Items that might have been seen advertised on television. It all stimulated the imagination, if only for a few moments.

National television offered special programing such as *Rogers and Hammerstein's Cinderella* and *Hallmark Hall of Fame* specials. There was the broadcast of *Macy's Annual Thanksgiving's Day Parade* and the landing of men on the moon. New Year's Eve was television movies with aliens or monsters. And there was the six o'clock news and now the endless reporting of the Vietnam War.

It seemed that our neighborhood was filled with children back then and everyone seemed to know each other, at least vaguely. Mr. J. worked at the potato chip factory. An older couple with grown children owned that brown, two-story house on the corner of Reber Avenue and Summit Street, with its manicured lawn and a nice, enclosed front porch. In the green-grass yard, flowers bloomed. A television might be heard through a screened door. It was a complacent place, unworried for the most part. Brick was never redder; paneling popular, Danish modern furniture was for sale at the furniture store downtown. The store that occupied a storefront off Mulberry Street with a second-floor open space filled with Walnut wood desks and dressers, new sofas and tables.

People in Waterloo, Iowa were barbers, sold used cars; made things. They sold *Avon, Tupperware* or *Amway* products. They were their mannerisms or hobbies. This one knits, he collects old bottles.

It was the 1960s. A sense of privacy had not been lost and you could still go to a place that was completely your own. You could

27

look to the future or the past, without serious thought. You were a part of the town and surrounding land and the larger idea of America. There was the quiet of a small town. The rudeness of noise.

A restaurant, the grocery store and retail stores were places where you would mix with other residents of Waterloo. You got a look at their clothes and what they bought. You had a sense of what was important to them and what was not. We were all affected by advertising, national news and the trends of the decade. Yet, we all reacted differently to the things around us. It was not online that we revealed our individual selves but in person. In public places and in our neighborhoods. We were all Americans and we were often more similar than we realized. A friendly conversation often revealed that fact. The weather shared on a day and the fall of night when we sought out that place called home.

As a community and a town, it was our American traditions that we had in common and the way we acknowledged holidays and the seasons. In ways that were necessary and individual as an expression of love or joy. Many of us went to a place of worship because of spiritual faith. There were losses and illness that did not touch us directly. Celebrations of marriage and birth and the end of life of those around us we loved or perhaps did not know. We shared the blue sky and rain and the first day of summer. That first day of snow and the color of the trees in autumn.

We shared colors; orange and brown, red and green, red, white and blue, black and old rose, pink or blue, the yellow of dandelions and the purple of violets. White and red carnations, roses, orange lilies, pink peonies, zinnias; orange and yellow marigolds. We also shared rhubarb, corn on the cob, string-beans, tomatoes, carrots and strawberries. Television, radio, advertising, consumer products, fads, pop culture, potluck suppers, picnics and fast food. Whatever was for sale or what we consumed. Our basic freedoms were the most individual thing we had to experience and the most commonly shared. Under the Iowa sky that was overcast or bright blue, we lived our lives.

It was the late 60s or early 70s. A VW beetle drove past us with vinyl flower decals on its windows. We drove past the new *Pizza Hut*, *McDonald's* with its golden arches, and the gas station with its store that sold seasonal items. This next to a new discount store named *K-Mart*. A *Beach Boys* song played on the car radio. The warm summer breeze let in through a half-open, back seat window.

You were in a car going to get bread and milk or running some other errand. On the way home, you passed the *Injun Country* park with its narrow trees and area for campers. I would think of those *Ford Mustangs* and *VW Karmann Ghia* cars in that grass-covered lot near the local grocery store, with convertible tops, leather seats and cool stick shifts. But the California inspired music had left the radio station and you were left with dusty cornfields growing on Midwest flat land. *Black Hawk Creek* in the wooded area and *Byrnes Park* with its measured flower beds and public swimming pool.

Lunch was American cheese, sliced ham with mayonnaise on *Wonder Bread*. A *Tupperware* glass of iced-tea. The gnats, bugs and bees above the weeds in the field made their noises above the tall grass rooted in the dry earth. The air was humid. The tree leaves silent today and the summer sky almost cloudless. The noise of a screen door being shut.

In the 1970s, a development of new, expensive homes sprang up on the Southwestern edge of our town, shadowing the elegant older homes of the Prospect Boulevard area. These houses on Prospect Boulevard were magnificent and still are. Large, well-built homes in a variety of styles on very large lawns. It was where my father found work putting on storm windows in the fall or screen windows in the spring. He also found work in other areas of Waterloo, like a giant of a house on the poorer East side of town. He would count out the windows, sometimes as many as twenty or more. An oval or attic window left out in the count. I would help him with these weekend jobs and he would pay me a percentage. It was really the only time we ever spent together.

Having returned as an adult and while living here, I was always conscious of the fact that my mother was no longer living; that my father had moved away from this place many years previous. It wasn't so much a conscious thought but an inner awareness of it. This was where they had raised me and now, I had returned for no real reason, unmarried, not having followed the usual traditions of society. I was unwed, detached from a church or any local group; mostly unknown in the community. I had returned to this place as a single, male adult with no real history attached to this place, except for my childhood and adolescence. But it was still home in every sense of the word and I made it so while I lived there. I revisited my youth. My walks to school in the bitter winter cold and snow. I listened to night sounds of crickets and thumping bugs against a screen door in the summer. Halloween came and Thanksgiving was celebrated with pumpkins and turkeys for sale at the local *Hy-Vee*. In spring, flowers bloomed alongside cracked sidewalks, dogs barked and bright green leaves appeared on the trees. Leaves that in the fall would cover lawns waiting to be raked into piles.

It had waited for me, this quiet place of brick elementary schools and churches and corner, used-car lots. I was that young man down the street with long blond hair, who had left for college. His departure announced with white sheet-cake and high school graduation cards; a carnation in his lapel.

I didn't realize at the time how much I would miss the rain soaked earth of this place, the crunch of snow and a parent returning on a cold winter's night from an errand. The time close to a holiday or a weekend. How rich the memory of the light of those rooms now seem. The incandescent glow of burnt orange glass from the dining room fixture. We came in shaking off snow from our shoes, carrying packages from the shopping mall or the grocery store, ingredients for

31

a Sunday dessert consisting of *Jell-O* and whipped cream and canned pineapple.

A big event in our town was the annual *National Dairy Cattle Congress,* a mixture of livestock show, exhibit and carnival held at the beginning of fall.

There were souvenirs to be had. Miniature sample loafs of *Wonder* white bread, brochures on new vacation trailers and pricey storm windows, salt water taffy, wood rulers, pens or pencils from the water softener company, balloons not inflated. At concession stands were hanging plastic bags of pink, blue and yellow cotton candy, overpriced hotdogs, one quarter, three-ball games of chance. It was the flash of sickly yellow fluorescent lights on amusement rides churning in the distant night, noise and sawdust alleys, strings of yellow lights, mooing cows, (big cows!), sheep and hogs, a proud 4-H farm kid on a magnificent horse. Blue ribbons were given out. People won prizes for things.

There were more refined exhibits like the garden and floral show. First Prize to Mrs. Wycoff for 'Asian Garden' a little card and blue ribbon might announce next to the floral arrangement. Mrs. Wycoff had won several times before.

I remember going one year with my mother and being embarrassed by a plump lady hollering out to the carnival audience on a tacky stage beckoning "the real men" to go behind the curtain for a peek at topless ladies.

"Here's where we separate the men from the boys!" she had announced into a squeaking microphone.

It had a carnival, farm equipment exhibits, livestock shows -lots of livestock shows. The color and movement of the event, the sounds, noise, and the blur of swirling yellow-colored fluorescent lights, the strings of lights, sawdust, dust, and the canvas tents is what made it so memorable. And it was affordable. And then it was over and the weather turned colder. The state fair in Des Moines was larger than our local, annual fair and yet it seems less memorable to me, only larger.

Halloween each year came the same as always. Orange colors and pumpkins at the grocery store for sale. The smell of hollowed-out pumpkins charred from candle flame; the feel of squashy pumpkin seeds in your hands. There were cardboard decorations to put up in the windows (not seen from indoors) with cats and ghosts with jack-o-lanterns. They were mixed with construction paper leaves traced from leaves collected on the way home from school. Leaves newly fallen, not dry and wind-blown as the ones that flanked sidewalks and covered yards. There was a house in our neighborhood on a nearby block that was newly renovated. Now a two-story modern box with *Pella* windows. Oh, what Halloween decorations they had one year! Giant carved pumpkins of every sort, scary, toothless, ghostlike expressions, ears and eyebrows. A scarecrow stuffed with straw. Orange lights around the windows. It looked crazy.

It was a Halloween night in Waterloo. The old brown-shingled house next door to ours looked empty. The old woman that lived there usually gave out sugar cookies with orange frosting and sprinkles in a wax-paper bag. This year it looked doubtful as there were no lights seen in the windows. A few kids wandered from house to house in costumes, the dime-store kind with colorful plastic masks. I was outside sitting on our side porch listening to the radio. Tonight, for Halloween, it was a broadcast of Orson Wells, *War of the Worlds*. The radio program began. It sounded silly and I wondered if people had really been that scared. Our carved pumpkin was fading again. The candle sputtering inside, then it went dark. Above, the leaves of the giant Cotton wood tree at the edge of our property made a sudden swooshing sound in the wind.

Thanksgiving weather was usually cold. Perhaps not snow, but frozen field ground. The weeds covered in frost. Gray and brown the same color, mostly gray the sky. Cold and better indoors however typical our celebration was. Yet, there was always the field behind our house. It was a place to escape to on a winter's afternoon; if snow had fallen, less so. The weed clumps mostly covered in drifts. Dry leaves caught in their stalks. It was flat and spacious. The trees at its edge. Barriers that only extended the imagination for their depth was shallow. Pine, oak and elm mostly and the underbrush of weeds.

While doing research on Waterloo, Iowa, I came across an aerial-view photograph (postcard image) of the *Rath Packing*

34

Company where my father had worked. It is a vintage image and the photograph looks retouched to enhance the image. The streets and surrounding area look bright and clean. But I remember the building and surrounding area as gray and cold-looking, an ugly, smelly, dark, brick-wall of a place. The main entrance façade of this plant was made of a red brick and several stories high. It cast a long shadow across the street that brought you to the entrance and exit. Whether on a bright, sunny summer afternoon or a gray winter morning, it always looked the same to me, a tall, imposing soot-covered, red brick wall casting its long angular shadow over the cars that passed by it. But once you left the area, drove across the rickety metal bridge that brought you to the West side of town, the natural light of day returned. Winter was winter and a sunny, summer day brought hope and the promise of something new. Driving away in a car, if you looked back you would see the smoke stacks of the plant in the distance, hear the rattle of the metal suspension bridge underneath us that we crossed on the way home, the sight of gray-brown trees along the banks of the Cedar River. We stopped for groceries. We never accepted charity.

My mother loved old movies and so did I. We loved the film music and the drama. Sometimes we stayed up too late to watch these old classic films on television, much to my father's dismay, as he always claimed to hear the set while he was trying to get a night's sleep. His day started very early at the packing plant. I recently saw the 1940 film, *Waterloo Bridge*, starring Vivien Leigh and Robert

Taylor. In the film, there is a wonderful scene with the two of them dancing to the song, *Auld Lang Syne*. It was just the sort of film we would have stayed up late to watch, disturbing my father's sleep.

We were Wesleyan Methodist. Our church, established in 1930, was first a wood structure painted white. The main sanctuary had bright stain glass windows and pews. A knotty-pine covering the walls of the adjacent space used for social functions and Sunday school. In the 1960s the church would be added on to. The exterior a light-colored brick and stone. The sanctuary was furnished in blond woods, garnet-red carpet, bronze and glass hanging light fixtures. Behind the alter hung a large wood cross, affixed to the pink cinder-block wall. The celebrations and ceremonies were typical, weddings, funerals, baby showers. A teen choral performed when there were enough teens. They even made a record. Each Mother's Day, we picked out a small plant for mom. At Wednesday night prayer meetings, missionaries came and gave presentations. There might be a slides show, objects from Sierra Leone or some other far away island, or South American place were displayed. My mother prayed fervently for these individuals, an endless reciting of names and missionary locations.

As I grew older the church congregation dwindled. Other Methodist churches had been built in Waterloo, new, larger churches with schools and church camp activities. Ours grew less favored, although a strong spiritual presence was always undeniable. The pew where the widows sat grew less occupied. Children grown had moved away. There were lots of reasons.

Chapter 3

_____

The dining room was the center of our house. It wasn't really a room but a corner of a room and open to our living room and kitchen. A kitchen counter with cupboards separated the kitchen from the dining room. The room was part of the small house's renovation and a new double, sliding window had been put in that gave us a view of our backyard and the field behind our house. At nightfall behind the field was a sunset. A rain storm brought a charcoal sky with random flashes of lighting. At night when the roll-type blinds were up, it framed a view of darkness. This window made the room a dramatic place, a place of seasons and passing time. It hosted birthday celebrations and graduations, holiday meals. It was a poor corner of a room, but it was magical at least to me as a child growing up. If it were summer, a plastic table cloth covered the table. Purple lilacs or peonies in a green glass vase might occupy the center. Tomatoes were brought in from the garden and placed there temporarily. It was a place where you witnessed tired parents after a long day's work, the faces of your siblings, neighbors down the street drinking coffee and sampling my mother's spice cake. Relatives had laid their gloves there, a gift for an occasion, greeting cards were displayed. It was just a table, but it was the center of the house. In older photographs, this room looks better. There is still a nice short brown carpet on the floor as opposed to vinyl linoleum. The Danish modern furniture is new along with the nice short, lined curtains on the windows. The walls are painted a bright mint green. In spring and summer, the sun never shined through this window as an elm tree left the backside of the house in shade. But there was the view of the grassy backyard and the field overgrown with weeds and it gave us a fresh breeze on certain days. In the far distance, a row of trees that edged the field hid a view of railroad tracks and the *Black Hawk Creek* wooded area. In winter, the view from this window was of a gray, cloudless sky. Snow and ice covered the field and trees. If a rain storm approached or tornado weather the sky outside this window gave us a warning. There was also the view of indoors through this window. At first a circular disk-shaped hanging fixture hung above the table. This would be replaced with another light fixture, one with burnt-orange colored glass shades, the fixture an early American style. These were small details, but they remained the same for many years. They are what framed holiday meals, celebrations, visits from relatives and neighbors. They framed nights when we sat studying for school or discussing a problem. It was a separate place on Thanksgiving and Christmas because it contained the table where we had our holiday meal. In this space was also a Danish modern breakfront, purchased at the same time of the renovation of the house. It matched the Danish modern dining table and chairs. In the top drawer of the breakfront were photo albums, these and table linens.

We had an *Eastman Kodak* Brownie camera that I think we used before buying an Instamatic. I think that is what it was called a *Kodak "Instamatic."* It had a flash that made our eyes red in the photographs.

The color of the photographs from the sixties had a certain color print to them and different from the film color of the seventies and eighties. In one photograph is my family sitting on our dark-green cut-velvet sofa against pale green living room walls. In another photograph, my mother is standing in front of our picture window in a brown dress with a wide orange -colored trim. These photographs must have been taken in the early seventies. In some of the photographs are parts of rooms like our kitchen or an area of the living room where we had a desk. How lucky that we captured these in photographs. Memories of holidays and celebrations returned; the warmth of the kitchen and the faces of friends and relatives. The time I sat at that desk with a typewriter and typed-out high-school graduation open-house invitations onto index cards. I put "graduation stickers" on them, a guy in a cap and gown, a diploma, etc. These were sent out to church members, friends and relatives. This was my task assigned by my mother, a good way to practice my typing.

The dining table was set with a large plate of lemon sugar cookies, foam coffee cups, paper napkins and a green-glass vase filled with purple lilacs. It was a breezy afternoon in May. Aunts and uncles would soon fill the room.

A cousin of mine who was in the Army at the time came one weekend for a visit. He sat at our dinner table in this room late at night talking with my father and mother - then only with his aunt, my mother, as my father had gone to bed. He was young and full of energy and as he talked, I listened staying near the edge of the room in the shadow of the kitchen. He became a part of the collective memory of that modest room that struggled for a superior identity, lifting itself up with a few collected treasures that occupied the shelves of the Danish-modern breakfront.

"You don't say" she would say quite amazed, with the black of night seen through the room's curtain-less window. She was like that, the same as earlier in the day, amazed by his every word. Then she would get up quickly to prepare coffee and a plate of store bought cookies.

He talked about the army and relatives. He talked about how history repeated itself and he gave us examples in American history. We looked at the photographs in our albums. Photographs of men in starched white shirts and felt hats. All the ladies in one photo -please, all come together for a day, a reunion, a visit. My mother's voice would be remembered by us, as she knew it would, like the evening itself, safe and incandescently lit by the circular-disk light fixture that hung from the ceiling in that room, measured by the clock, the room dark at the edges. This half-room wasn't just a space, but a place to create a mood. It might be a struggle but with effort – imagination, it became more. A limited drama confined to the light in the room and at times it was magic.

It was a dining room, but it was also a place for stories of relatives and events faintly remembered like a black and white blurred photograph. It was births and death. It was American history. It was stories of places where people had grown up. It was red, white and blue, Uncle Sam, courage and sentiment, unwavering patriotism, something similar to faith but involving laws of a different sort. Patriotism was something you were taught and remembered on a July 4th holiday, that feeling you felt when a marching band passed you in a parade on a day of celebration. It was vanilla ice cream and a bit of cake-equal and fair. It was as American as apple pie.

In one photograph of my family and our Sunday dinner guests, we are seated around the table in this room. You can see the view through the window of our backyard and the open field that lay beyond. It is winter, perhaps late afternoon or early evening, a short winter day. In the fading daylight, the snow covering the ground looks a colorless white, a cold white snow with a surface brittle in places. The trees branches are bare. In another photograph, I am standing near the table in this room. I am a child of perhaps six. I look very blond and blue-eyed. I am wearing a new blue and white sweater that buttons at the front.

Included in those photo albums were there were those annual elementary school photos. I wore my new cowboy shirt from *Ward's* one year, in the single, color photos we ordered of me. The shirt was blue and red and had a gold ribbon design sewn into it. One of your homeroom class was for sale, this an 8 x 10 black and white glossy or matte print.

On the day of my parent's thirty-fifth wedding anniversary to be held at our Church parsonage, I quickly retrieved a few photographs from the breakfront top drawer to display at a party planned by my younger sister and myself. There weren't enough photographs to view it seemed and people asked for more. How I wish now I had put up more photographs. Made more of an effort. They were so grateful at the time. How simple yet important it seemed later. After my mother had passed away I rifted through our many photographs and thought of it. It was one of those things you tried not to regret.

There was the gathering place in a house. Your mother's cooking, visits from relatives, refrigerated carnations in a box that were worn to a wedding, left over pot roast and potatoes wrapped in tin foil in the refrigerator. The early winter frost on the edge of a window, fireflies and thunder that never sounds the same as it did. The green-grass yard flooded in a rain storm and the smell of freshly ironed linens. We grow older and forget until some event, some emotion brings them back for a moment. The smell of pink peonies, the slender green stems of the orange tiger lily, the sour taste of rhubarb, sliced garden tomatoes with table salt. They are worth remembering and writing about.

Chapter 4

After a Sunday after-church noon dinner, the attic of our house (my room) was where I could be found. Several unopened books were stacked on my desk reminding me that I had not done my homework. This always seemed the case and l carried a dreadful guilt along with the books. The walls of the room were angled to accommodate the roof and the floor covered with ugly diamond-pattern linoleum I had partially covered with rugs. The furniture in the room consisted of a bed, desk, dresser with mirror and an old console radio. The dresser mirror was too tall for the room and was tilted forward, uselessly reflecting the opposite wall and floor. The radio was a *General Electric*. I had read the manufacturer's information many times on the inside cabinet door that concealed the face and dials. It had been purchased at a yard sale. On top of the radio was my collection of bottles, different shapes of pale-green and amber that once held medicine, vanilla or vinegar and with trademarks identifying the brand. The sound of static grew louder as the radio warmed and I dialed through channels hearing familiar pop tunes or an occasional radio voice, then no sound at all -only static. Switching back to FM, the music returned and I settled on a local station that broadcast soft rock like *Lobo* or *Crosby, Stills and Nash*. As was my habit, I sat in front of the radio listening. Heat poured through the floor vent and the room, usually too cold, was now too hot. It was winter in Northern Iowa and although snow had yet to fall, cold and shorter days marked the season. I decided to leave the house and walk. I pulled on a sweater and my outdoor jacket and made way down the small noisy attic steps. Once outside I headed for the open field directly behind our house. I broke off several stems of brittle dry milkweed. The pods still held cottony white seeds that fluttered in the wind as I walked. Now only the smooth empty brown pods remained. This narrow trail through grass and weeds ended at a group of trees. I had dressed in layers with a sweater and flannel shirt under my jacket but still felt the cold along my arms and shoulders. The top part of my gloveless hands, numb and red. I walked heavily around the leaf-covered ground listening with satisfaction. This open field of land seemed to belong to no one. So, claimed by me a long time ago when I was a boy, pushing through tall grass with great purpose and no reason. I looked up to see the sunlight shift among the trees. There was only stillness and a strange, shifting pattern of sunlight.

Now more conscious of the cold, I turned the collar of my jacket up around my ears and headed back towards the house. It was now closer to early evening as I approached our yard and I could see a light through a window of the house. As I entered the house smelled of cinnamon and my mother was in the kitchen placing squares of cake onto a plate. She seemed pleased that I had ventured out, even on this cold and overcast day. I felt odd and it was always like this on a Sunday when I was growing up, something out of place; melancholy.

When I was a boy I remember playing with the parts of a broken transistor radio and a science kit. The science kit consisted of test tubes with simple experiments. With these and with a block of wood and a toy train remote I made an imaginary invention. It didn't do anything -but yet it did. For some reason, I had the knowledge that if I believed it did, then it did and that was what was important. If I believed it was a communicating device, then on some level it was. I think as adults we often forget to dream what is possible.

Chapter 5

We knew the names of our neighbors. The Browns and the Smiths. There was the neighbor couple that owned the comer grocery. Their son had been killed in the Vietnam War. It saddened us so. And there was the divorcee, middle-aged neighbor woman who worked nights as a barmaid to support her two slightly disfunctional children.

Another one of our neighbors, handsome Mr. Varmer, gave us empty cigar boxes that smelled of aromatic Cuban tobacco.

Old Mrs. McHenry down the street was Irish and she had hair as white as snow. Her son seldom came home to visit as he lived far away and so she sat on the cement porch of her tiny house on cool summer evenings talking with the neighbor children.

We experienced things with these neighbors that we hardly knew. The street that we lived on. A national news event on television that affected us as Americans. We grew older with them. We adapted to the changing world. They became a peripheral part of our identity. We viewed the larger world as a place we could not fully respond to. Even when we were angry at, mourned or celebrated a thing common to all of us. But our opinions were as important as any other. Our country and the property of land we lived on and owned.

Chapter 6

There is a neighbor I haven't mentioned that I will tell you about now.

Just over the line of my father's property, on the side of the white post fence he had erected one summer, stood a giant of a cotton wood tree, a giant even for a cotton wood, and very near this giant tree stood a big, ramshackle, two-storied, brown-shingled house. In winter ice clung to these brown tar-shingles making them sparkle in the daylight. The house was old, built probably in the twenties or thirties and a bit run-down, but I was glad it was still there because it was so different from the rest of the newer neighborhood. It had remained like an unexpected cool afternoon breeze on a hot summer day. There was no mystery to the rest of our neighborhood. Here there was mystery and history. The backyard was overgrown with tall sedge grass and weeds but also flowers and flower bushes and there was an old rectangular-shaped wood shed-coop and a garage with a sloping roof. These were bare of any paint or repair and had weathered to a dark gray. The cotton wood tree, too large, had outgrown our newly renovated neighborhood. But all of this would be gone in a few years. The lot cleared and neatly covered with landfill.

The owner of this property was our neighbor, a Mrs. Janson, who was herself well past the age of retirement but still went to work each day at a nursing home where she had been employed for many years. A silhouette of a shape with her small shoulders and back arched forward, she had taken on the same curvy lines of the old black 1940s *Chevy Deluxe* she drove each day to work. Her white hair was a stark contrast to the shabby-looking, old black wool coat she always wore but blended nicely with the snowy weather and billowy car exhaust that rose from the back of her car as it warmed up in the mornings.

In the evenings, I could see her through her tall kitchen window near the back of the house carrying a kettle or pan. It was the light from this window that I remember. A single electric bulb hung from the room's ceiling that lit up the interior of the old kitchen at night. It's faded yellow walls, the big, old-fashioned white porcelain sink, the pots and pans that hung from a wood shelf, a row of tin canisters that lined that shelf. It was a view from the past and like the old-fashioned flowers that grew in her yard; cream-colored lily of the valley, pink bleeding hearts and the green and mauve-colored jack-in-the-pulpit. Outside the shed, I had found a rusted sickle, farm tools, a half-rotted pitchfork, the metal part of it, square-shaped and sturdy. On windy fall days, the place looked melancholy. Drifting winter snow brought a contrast of cold to the warmth of light cast from the tall windows of the house.

But it was the cotton wood tree I noticed the most. Another smaller tree near our yard, a maple, dropped sticky seeds that stuck to our good shoes on Sunday mornings. But I always associated the maple seeds that fluttered down with the cotton wood tree. It had engulfed the maple tree with its size.

On summer days, I would stand beneath the cotton wood tree listening to the thousands of leaves of its wide-branch crown rustling in the wind, prior to a rainstorm or just a day. The tree's leaves shimmered slightly against the dark blue and charcoal of the sky.

There was a day or perhaps it was a culmination of days when a rain storm approached, and the sky grew as dark as charcoal. Not at first but slowly. Scattered lighting filled the sky and the rumbling of thunder. The giant cotton wood tree near our house would catch the increasing wind. Then it would rain or perhaps the wind would blow harder, and then quiet down again, the sky clearing. In winter, the tree's bare branches were half-white with snow. On other days, the tree seemed lifeless. Its leaves and branches moving high above in soundless slow motion, gray bark-covered branches blocking the sun, its shadow engulfing the tree itself. The giant cotton wood tree could predict a storm. Every leaf on the tree motionless and silent or the trees branches frantic in the wind. It told you something even in the way it cast its own shadow. Its branches might move ever so slightly on a warm spring day. The new green leaves not completely grown. It didn't really change color like other trees during the fall months but drop its leaves and twigs all the same as winter approached. Perhaps it had seen more seasons than us.

It was the fall season of that year. I was now a teenager. One day the brown- shingled house suddenly seemed to be empty and old

Mrs. Janson gone. A piece of paper on the front of the house told us it was to be condemned. The curvy, black car she had driven was gone as well. The windows of the house were soon boarded up with sheets of fresh plywood that advertised the local lumberyard. A few days later I discovered in the farm shed behind the house a few pieces of furniture. A floor lamp with a marble base, and a narrow dresser mirror with an ornate carved-wood frame. The mirror, cloudy and rusty at its edges caught the afternoon sunlight from a dusty window.

Men from the city now inspected the old house and I knew it would soon be torn down. With a sense of urgency, I told a classmate at school about the tree and the abandoned house. As I related my story I tried to find a balance between reality and exaggeration. I told him about old Mrs. Janson's black wool coat, the old car she drove to work each day, the oranges electric candles she put in the windows of her house at Christmas, the crumbly Halloween sugar cookies with orange sprinkles she gave out in wax-paper bags instead of store-bought candy, and the antiques most probably sitting in one of the sheds outback of the house. He seemed mostly interested in the antiques. And so, we agreed to meet after school and walk to the old house.

As we turned the corner onto our street what my new friend saw first was the cotton wood tree.

"It's not so big," he stated flatly. My heart now sank a bit.

"And they should tear that house down!" he said with scorn.

51

We had trouble getting the door of the shed open but with the two of us pushing hard against the wood slat door it finally creaked open making an arching line in the dirt.

"Nothing but junk" he said, and with that my friend promptly headed for home and I was left to close the shed door and secure its lock-less, rusty hinge with the top part of an old rake.

What was it he had missed? That stuff was not junk! I thought to myself. I climbed the stairs to my attic room and waited for the dinner of pork chops and potatoes my mother had announced when I had first entered our house.

The next day thunder was heard in the cloudy sky. Then distant flashes of lightening. The leaves of the cotton wood tree rustled a warning of rain. The blowing wind causing them to sweep to one side of the sky. Then the rain drops began to fall. Causing the caked dust on the ground to turn to mud.

A few weeks later, men from the city arrived and it became evident that the old house and farm shed was to be torn down that week. After they left the property, I quickly removed the items that I wanted from the farm shed behind the house, dragging the stuff onto the tall, unmoved grass in the back yard. This a dresser's mirror and a shade-less floor lamp.

That next afternoon I watched from our porch steps as the exposed, pale-colored wallpapered wails of the upstairs rooms of the old house disintegrated into plaster dust. The bare, exposed wood stairs and railing now leading to only sky and clouds and producing a memory of the afternoon my mother ran out of vanilla while baking. She did not mention Mrs. Janson often, only waved to her from time to time and I knew it must be an emergency by the desperation in her voice and by the flour on her apron. After knocking on Mrs. Janson's door and explaining the purpose of my errand I was led inside of the front room of the house. Mrs. Janson disappeared into the kitchen in search of the stuff. She soon returned with a red and white box of *Schillings* and I expressed my mother's appreciation. We said our goodbye on the tiny front porch she had managed to recently add to the front of the old house, the lumber on the thing still unpainted after several months. I had gotten a look at the place inside, faded floral wallpaper, a wall shelf with several framed photographs and a dimly-lit floor lamp with a nice silk shade. Its light reflecting off the shiny, varnished, dark-wood stair railing and steps that led to a shadowy second floor. Those same steps now led to the Halloween evening I sat on our porch listening to *War of the Worlds* on our portable radio. This a re-broadcast of an old radio program about a tale of space men invading earth that had not sounded real to me at all. How could people have believed such nonsense! Looking up, I could see the cotton wood tree's large branches swaying back and forth in the night wind, high above our house as if listening as well.

With the old house now gone, the cotton wood tree seemed out of sorts with the neighborhood. It was out-of-scale with the newly-built, rectangle houses and yet it wanted to remain, to observe the new changes to the neighborhood. That summer a mass of orange lilies and big, white and dark pink peonies stubbornly bloomed next to an imaginary house and shed.

It was on a humid day many years later; a visit home, that I found the cotton wood tree gone as well. My father had expressed his joy with a newly-built fence painted a fresh white marking our property line. The tree was gone and our house looked naked on its small, shade-less lot now properly joined with the other houses in the neighborhood but leaving me to mourn its loss. I was surprised by my own sadness, surprised at how affected I was by the loss of this tree and I walked to where it had stood but found no shade.

The cotton wood tree is still visible, but only at certain times of the day. Just as daylight starts to fade or a cloud covers the sun producing a familiar shadow. Its language of wind-rushing crescendos never quite matched by any other tree and only heard at times of brief, rare silence.

A new housing addition went up across the street from our house. I watched as they were built. First the cement basement appeared, next, the finished first floor covered in clean plywood sheets, then the frame of the house marking the small rooms. Soon the rectangular box house was finished with new windows that had stickers still attached to them. These were one-story, two-bedroom houses in a choice of pastel colors. The new owners, mostly young couples planted their yards with shrubs and flowers from *K-Mart's* greenhouse. Behind these houses, several other homes were built around a circular courtyard. These were a bit larger and one or two had a split level. Two-by-fours and plywood scraps were available for the asking. The boys in the neighborhood played army around the mud yards of the houses as they were being built. I built myself a fort in the tall weeds of the field behind our house. This attached to the trunks of two small trees.

Gone was Mrs. Jansons's brown-shingled house and the shed building. Gone was the giant cotton wood tree.

The elm trees in our front and back yard would die of Dutch-elm disease. Now only the tall, scraggly pine tree that edged our property remained with its small pine-cones barely reachable. When the sun shone, it glared down on us and after it rained, there were no trees shaking off the rain drops or warning us of a change in weather. Here is an imagined story with the old brown-shingled house as the setting. This last remaining vestige of a neighborhood more rural and from another era always seemed a part of the past and imaginary at times.

May Janson, A Story

The month was a November and the year was 1932. May Janson and her three children now occupy the kitchen of their house. It was an old two-story, brown-shingle covered house with an acre and a half of land. The kitchen was the only room in the house with any heat. The source of this precious heat was a wood stove that was now burning corn cobs. There was timber behind the house along the edge of a field, but they dare not cut it as it belonged to a neighbor. Corn cobs were all they had to burn, these from the corn they had grown that past summer on their own land.

May's husband, Frank had gone to look for work. He had hitched a ride with a man going East to Dubuque, Iowa. May had made up a bed for herself and the two girls in the kitchen. The boy named Henry, now ten years old was to sleep at the edge of the kitchen in the hallway on a thin feather mattress. He would be the coldest, but it couldn't be helped.

After they had finished a supper of bread and potato soup, May and her children sat at the wood table in the kitchen listening to the radio. The radio show was a program of music and clever talk. The folks on it sounded carefree. The Friday evening show was different each week. May liked the orchestra music the best and the songs that were sung by men and women with the loveliest of voices, crooners and sopranos.

"How about some apples?" Henry asked.

"There for a winter Sunday meal," replied Bess with irritation.

"Stop complaining in front of your sisters. Do you hear them complaining?"

"I am not complaining. I just asked that's all."

The tablecloth covering the kitchen table had a pattern of bright red apples on it. Apples they could not eat. The picked apples that they had left were in a few *Ball* canning jars in the cellar. One light bulb hung above the table and burned defiantly despite the lack of money to pay for it. This and the electric radio were a luxury they could no longer afford. The winter wind whistled about the old house. Snow lay on the ground outside. With Frank gone, May was afraid of vagrants or worse, but she would never mention it to the children. They would go to bed soon. Sleep was an escape from hunger and idleness, but idleness was the work of the devil. It was a Saturday and they would all find something to do the following day. She would wait for Frank to return. He might find work. She hoped he would. There was talk of railroad work in Illinois, closer to Chicago. As she listened to a radio commercial, she thought of the things she had on a shelf in the living room. China pieces that she might have sold the year before but now things seemed so bad that she knew it would be useless to try. The main street of their small town was deserted almost, except for the soup kitchen, the few retail stores that remained and the bank-post office. Even the doctor had abandoned his downtown office for his own house. She didn't feel bad for herself, but she was scared. She was scared even now as she listened to the music of the radio show that seemed a happy world away.

Chapter 7

My father was good at building things, like fences. He went hunting in the fall. I do not remember if it was early fall or closer to winter but he would go hunting for pheasants. He would bring the dead birds back to the house and lay them on a newspaper in the basement before they were plucked and prepared for cooking.

You could smell the blood of the bird. I still remember this smell.

I remember going downstairs to where the birds lay. I walked over to them and examined one of them closely and cautiously. The feathers on the bird were one of the most beautiful things I had ever seen. I marveled at the iridescent colors of the feathers. They were magnificent and at that moment I hated my father for having killed such a beautiful living thing.

In my mind I understood that to hunt and kill was a manly thing to do. It was what a normal man did and without any real remorse or at least any lasting remorse. Obviously, I wasn't a man in this sense and the idea bothered me. So, I hid. I stayed closer to my mother or occupied my time alone. I fiercely hung on to my memory of the sight of that bird and somehow that had saved it from death.

The *Rath* meat-packing plant where my father worked was hardly ever mentioned, almost never, and the modest existence that my parents had created, home and family was never invaded by the mention of his exhausting job. Except for perhaps at bedtime when my father feared a lack of sleep. The packing plant remained remote in my mind; a dark-bricked, foul-smelling wall of a place attached to cold and windy, winter mornings or a humid, late afternoon in summer. Just the purchasing of groceries after picking my father up at the plant, cold milk, bread and more, was an escape from the place. A belief in God, the reality of a God, helped balance it all.

Multi-colored plastic flags and a hand-lettered sign advertised the event that was about to begin this very day on the *Whittier* Grade School grounds, the annual, *Whittier* Ice Cream Social. A long row of tables were set up and covered with rolls of crisp, white paper tablecloth and beautiful cakes of every sort. These were cakes baked and brought by the grade-school students moms, cakes of every sort', fluffy white cakes with coconut frosting, lemon cake, chocolate cakes, angel food, devil's food, *Betty Crocker* and spongy cakes, cakes with maple sugar frosting and simple quick white-cakes with wavy pink frosting. The very same cakes the artist-painter, Wayne Thiebaud might paint. The ice cream flavors scooped out at the end the tables were chocolate and vanilla.

At one end of the schoolyard were rows of chairs in a semi-circle where the school band was to play. Games of chance were to be held like count the beans in the jar (I actually won this one year) or spinning a wheel for a prize. Moms in nice dresses and frilly starched aprons, dads cleaned up. A breeze or sometimes the terrible

59

threat of rain, Mulberry and Elm trees shading the school grounds. This year the weather was perfect. What year, I do not recall. Just a year of fine spring-like weather. My parents always attended but I would arrive first then after my father had cleaned up he would arrive with mom.

One year it rained, and the event was held in the school's gymnasium basement, noise and laughter ringing off the gymnasium walls. It wasn't the same but at least it wasn't canceled.

Recently I "Googled" *Whittier Grade School* and a photograph of a renovated *Whittier School* came up. The old building a landmark now and converted into residences although it basically looks the same on the outside, a handsome, renaissance two story brick and concrete building. There was also another response to this search, an obituary notice for my 1st Grade teacher at *Whittier* who had died just a few days prior. She had the good fortune to live until her nineties. I remember her as a slender, handsome woman with dark hair and red lipstick. She was firm and yet kind and you didn't mess with her, a tough lady to the end.

Chapter 8

Mrs. A. was in her late fifties, wore eyeglasses with a green tint and had a face made of dough. Her manner was practical and most of the time she seemed pleasant enough. She spoke up when necessary expressing herself as she should. And her appearance was as neat as one of her knitting projects. She still worked but was nearing retirement age. My father drove her to work, to the same meat packing plant where he worked and where a good percentage of Waterloo's labor force worked. In the evenings and on weekends, she worked on her small knitting and sewing projects. These were soaps covered in netting and sequins that resembled fish, embroidered hand towels, baby clothes for church shower gifts, and aprons as wedding gifts. She might even knit a sweater or a kaftan using a soft rainbow-colored yarn she liked. She collected cups and saucers and souvenir spoons. Mr. and Mrs. A. had purchased a movie projector and screen when the children had been quite young and had purchased travel-log films through a company that specialized in such films. These were travel films of Europe mostly, the scenic Swiss Alps, excursions through Denmark or Germany, the hilly, green countryside of Ireland or the romance of France.

Mr. A. was now retired and seemed to busy himself with errands and house- related projects. He was a master at creating small dramas relating to these projects and this was the fodder for opinions and carefully reached conclusions later shared with my parents. He was very judicial regarding these reached conclusions as if to reassure us they were undeniable truths.

"Now this is the way I see it," he would say officially, stating an unshakable opinion, "and here's a copy of today's paper as I promised."

There was something quiet and timeless about the first-floor rooms of the A's house, impenetrable and safe from the outside world. The high-ceiling living room had been painted a soft pale green and in one corner of this front room was a reading lamp positioned toward an overstuffed chair that cast a bright glow of light that dimly lit the whole room. White curtains that looked shear but almost opaque covered the windows and were framed with heavy-looking, nice floral drapes. A narrow, half-enclosed stairway leading to the upstairs of the house was uninviting and resigned you to the space below. From this same front room space was a wide entryway that opened to a small dining room. The chairs around the dining room table were perfectly positioned. A white porcelain plate of carefully stacked *Oreo* cookies had been placed in the center of this table. These were for the A's invited guests, neighbors, the same guests they often had over for coffee and cookies during the early evening hours -this just after supper and no later as Virginia rose at 5am for the day shift at the plant. The house's kitchen, only partially visible from the dining room, was large and old-fashioned. The kitchen walls were built-in cupboards as high as the ceiling itself. A circular fluorescent fixture in the ceiling of the room cast a utilitarian, sensible bright light onto the space that seeped into the dining room when clicked on. The A's invited guests, Mr. and Mrs. Bland had arrived and now both couples were seated at the dining table chatting. The pungent smell of fresh coffee from a stainless- steel percolator percolating in the kitchen filled the rooms. Mrs. Bland munched on an *Oreo* cookie while Virginia explained to her a knitting project unfolded on the dining-room table in front of the two women. The two men discussed, Mr. A. doing most of the talking and Mr. Bland gave a thoughtful nod from time to time.

Mr. and Mrs. A. had captured something about us. Perhaps it was simply our attention. Their home movie of us as children, their visits and my parent's alternate visits for coffee and cookies, sometimes an evening meal. They were what we were not; another point of view, opinions, projects and newsy chat and they were like the *Oreo* cookies they offered when we came for a visit neatly stacked on a plate, an affordable treat and somehow tied to the rattling motion and sound of their home-movie projector. That miracle of light and jumpy images that came out of their Kodak machine with its big gray-metal reels of film, this mostly footage from saved-for tour vacations or of their own two children, as children. They were tied to the things in their house, delicate knick-knacks and houseplants in their windows that filled pieces of green-glazed pottery', the short wool-patterned rug on their living room

63

floor that never showed a stain.

They were typically Midwestern in every way. They dressed down sensibly for hard work and looked modestly successful when it was necessary. They found humor in simple things and approached everything with practicality. They were religious and protestant. They had grown older and their children were now adults. They attended church services less often. It was an appearance they made at church. They were fussy at times, with each other, and they could be a mild annoyance. Showing up at inopportune times when our house was a mess or my parents were tired and expecting a Sunday afternoon nap. They showed up at the Bland's home for birthdays and graduations too and could always be relied upon for an appearance and an introduction to relatives. They were neater than us, settled and uncluttered, our good friends and neighbors.

Chapter 9

———————

For many years my grandmother lived at the Polk County Home in Des Moines, IA., now demolished. A large brick building with huge screened-in porches and long rooms filled with rows of beds. The second facility and last place she lived in was a standard nursing home with TV room and dining room.

I found traces of her in a drawer in our basement. A jewelry box with rhinestone brooches in an art-deco style. Old-fashioned buttons removed from a dress or coat. Even a letter or two.

On that day, she was wearing a navy-blue cotton dress. Most of the time we would find her in one of the stretchy pants suits my mother had bought for her but today was unusually warm. Her straight silver hair was always combed back in a pageboy style, neatly cut to one length and behind her ears. Of Dutch descent, she was still beautiful even as an older woman. Her hands were graceful and expressive. I had seen photographs of her as a young girl smartly dressed in suits and hats, standing next to the other Hudson sisters. My mother never spoke of her past and I often wondered what had happened to her as a young girl and why she had been unable to care for herself at such an early age. I never knew my grandfather but what I didn't know I made up. A drinker and a vaudevillian of sorts I had been told. And so, his image appeared to me in old movies and a few stories told by my mother. And as an adult I realized that he must have had a good head of hair and for this I am eternally grateful.

My grandmother elaborated on what sounded like an uneventful week as my mother embellished this empty telling with exaggerated approval. My grandmother had a grace and she conveyed this grace simply, in her genuine smile, her conveyance of love -after all this was all she really had to give us. I was aware of it vaguely though and was silently offended when my father would laugh at her, watching her walk from the car with my mother back into the old, state-run nursing home where she lived.

It was the end of the day and another Iowa sunset was setting in the surrounding fields. But this sunset was different. Different in the way it was colored and how it filled the whole scene before us with brilliant, dimming sunlight, a silver and orange glowing light that brimmed at the horizon and was mixed with the pink of the sky and lingering gray clouds. In the safety of the yard my sister and I looked out at this picturesque view in silence. We had been to this place before, the house of a relative in a nearby Iowa town. It was the kind of house that seemed to belong to a larger piece of land like a farmhouse might be. But it was located in a very small town. The inside rooms of the house were paneled and shadowy in places. The adults were seated at the kitchen table talking, reminiscing, and the light of the bare, kitchen light-bulb growing brighter and harsher against the fading light of day seen through a kitchen window. A place never looked more rural after nightfall.

Chapter 10

The downtown Waterloo I remember no longer exists. But I have written about it and here it is, hopefully dished up as well as that hamburger platter at *Woolworth's l*unch counter with a generous side of sliced dill pickles and salty potato chips.

The department store was *J. C. Penny*. When you got off the elevator on Level 5 (there was a ding) you were in the ladies hat department. It was quite fashionable with swiveling oval-shaped mirrors atop small tables and backless chairs where you could sit and try on the hats. The hats shellacked rounds with wisps of veils or pastel pillbox shapes with soft feathers and netting. Others more like bonnets -or summery straw hats decorated with brightly colored flowers fashioned from the same woven straw. The famous fashion designer *Halston* was designing hats about this time, his most famous being the pillbox shape.

On level 5 there was a fabrics department as well with pattern books to select from. One sleepy afternoon I remember vividly. My mother sorting through *McCall's* sewing patterns with me nowhere to wander but through the racks of women's fluffy wool coats. It was as dull as the remembered afternoon-time my mother ironed clothes with the soap opera, *As The World Turns* on TV.

On another floor of *J.C. Penny* was a toy department that sometimes was of interest. And on another floor, there was a back-counter area for gift-wrapping with samples of store boxes wrapped in wonderful paper and clipped bows you immediately coveted. It was on this floor that I would purchase a *Westmoreland* milk-glass dish for my mother, a stemmed candy dish with an apple motif.

One fall, my mother took me here to buy school clothes. This was very unusual as I usually got one piece of clothing at a time. Dad must have received a better check from the packing plant. That fall it was corduroys in gold and green colors and matching long- sleeve, patterned knit shirts, socks and underwear. All of this bought in the Boys Department in the basement. The first day of school I wore my new clothes, but they seemed too new, too bright and I suppose not cool. But I really didn't care for some reason. I liked my new clothes. They were soft and comfortable -and I just didn't care anymore.

Across from the department store was a dime store with a long lunch counter.

This was the best thing about this place. Glass coolers offered bubbling fruit-drink. The plastic-covered menu offered chicken salad on white bread with a side of sliced pickle, salty potato chips and a syrupy *Coca-Cola*. This snaking counter seemed endless, practically the length of the store. There was a *Kodak* counter with those big photo ads of vacationing families.

There were aisles of notions, lots of dime store stuff, quick buys and every holiday celebrated with candy, decorations -whatever appropriate. Shiny green shamrocks, lacey pink valentines and red jelly candies, boxed chocolate-covered cherries and strings of

Christmas twinkle lights blinking in their boxes. Colors like fake green grass and chocolate malt-ball Easter eggs. And greeting cards, religious, get well, birthday, with our sympathy...

On the East side of town, on the other side of the Cedar River there was a neon dragon on the facade of the corner Chinese restaurant that blinked off and on. It looked wonderful on a rainy day. Inside were booths and Chinese paper lanterns with red tassels hanging from the ceiling. Carved wood screens divided the booths in places. The walls were half-covered with mirrors. It looked far-eastern, sort of. Later this place would become something else; almost empty. I don't recall but I remember the wallpaper, images of Paris, France, poodles and wrought iron chairs, cafes with stripped canopies.

A rather humorous thing about our small mid-western downtown was that it had a bit of New York influence. On the East-side of town there was *New York Fashions*, a posh ladies dress-shop on Mulberry Street with *New York Fashions* in big, fancy script letters. There was even a Park Avenue. *Larry's,* a men's clothing store was owned by a Jewish man named - Larry! This place was great because the clothes were always on sale. This was now during the early seventies and Larry tried to carry cool stuff like wild-patterned shirts, bell-bottoms, long double-breasted coats and Nehru jackets. At my senior prom I wore a shiny, black, double-breasted silk suit I had bought at *Larry's*. *Wards Department Store* on the West side of downtown was a cramped space. The merchandise square footage was limited to two small floors. Tools were next to work shirts and winter coats. It was here that my mother had bought me a western-style shirt. I really loved this shirt. It had red panels and fancy western embroidery across the front of the shirt. I was never prouder than when I wore this shirt. My mother told me this as an adult -something not really remembered by myself.

"You wanted that shirt so badly." she told me.

Early Summer

I was wearing my maroon-striped pullover-long-sleeved with the groovy, long lapels, this and a pair of bell-bottom jeans, the kind with light-color stitching that made them look cool. It was my first year of high school and the beginning of summer. I searched for new ways to occupy my summer days. There were my yard jobs, working in a garden or mowing a lawn. A package of *Doritos* and a quart of *Pepsi* was my way of expressing my new, temporary financial freedom. The library was still a source for books. At school, there had been rumors of corn de-tasseling jobs that sounded arduous if not nearly impossible to complete, yet financially rewarding. Not for me I decided. I now walked to nowhere on this early summer day, warm and sunny. A bright blue sky framed by the green leaves of trees. I reached Third Avenue, a street several blocks from ours, parallel to our tar street, a nicer, wider street shaded with trees, no one's history and lined with modest wood houses. I continued my walk, the neighborhood so quiet you could hear the faint breeze in the trees; a car passing slowly on the way to a destination or home. Now I had reached the edge of an even nicer neighborhood where the upper-middle class resided with larger lawns and cone or circular-trimmed evergreens. There was nowhere to go, to walk too really, no sidewalk and this place was tied only to random memories. Of a storm-window job my father had done nearby. A ride home from high school or the mall. There was the house of the rich doctor's son that also attended my high school. (Many years later and at a distance, I would see this high school classmate in the lobby of a Broadway theater before a performance.) This more elegant residential area of Waterloo represented good colonial America and their slowly acquired tastes. They had earned more than us, were more deserving, or just plain lucky we might have quickly guessed. My mother once declared that she was happy for what she had but I couldn't help realizing her disappointment at such a very small house with its shallow, sloping backyard that edged a field of weeds. I returned home to our street, our very small white, wood house with its charcoal-colored window shutters and abbreviated front yard. A place with sea-foam-green walls and a brown-speckled carpet bought on sale, that didn't look too bad.

The results of consumerism were before us. The *Campbell's Tomato Soup* and *Saltine Crackers* that we ate for lunch. The Easter Sunday clothing purchased at *Montgomery Ward* or *J.C. Penny* ready to be worn to church. The new portable *Zenith* transistor radio purchased at the electronics store. We had filled the *Ford* car's tank with gas from the *Standard Oil* or *Shell* gas station. *Standard Oil* gave out free decals that I put on my school-book covers.

I had assembled a cardboard Apollo II from a kit which I had purchased from somewhere. I kept the newspaper clippings of this historic event from the *Waterloo Daily Courier*. A full two-page spread with spectacular photographs.

What was familiar was American to us. The fast food restaurants, the department store chain and the name brands advertised on television. These things mattered but not as much as spiritual salvation, simple kindness or hard work. If you were from Iowa, hard work was your calling card. You got things done and well. Thoroughness was part of being Iowan and American. You wouldn't have that modest house or new car without them. Or that family with good kids going out for sports, cheerleading or the debate team at school.

There were those iconic symbols from this era. Vinyl peace signs and pop-art flowers on the windows of VW vans and beetles. Even the *Hallmark Store* at the *Crossroads Mall* now carried versions of pop-art and psychedelic groovy posters. With poems and doves of peace on them. Lite-rock music played on the radio. Another *Pizza Hut* had opened on University Avenue.

Chapter 11

During that time, the early 1970s, Waterloo, Iowa had adapted to the times. It went from refrigerated white carnations to mums, yellow and almost scentless. A disappointment never expressed as the loss was too great. The sixties to present day not fully remembered; forgiven mostly. The world place was framed by television, radio; the six-o'clock news as if we were outside of it. Outside of something not purchased, something on a rack like a cool shirt we didn't buy, but only looked at. We were more apart of small things like greetings cards and the ordinary luxury of those orange lilies that bloomed along our backyard fence. In winter, when the earth was frozen, rock hard it seemed and covered with snow frost, even as a child you realized the limits of the place. You noticed the wooded edges of the field behind your father's house. And the dry stalks of weeds and tall grass held the answers to what was beyond a question not needing to be answered at all, for the sun was no longer hiding behind clouds in the sky. And then your daydreams stopped.

Birthdays were remembered as if to tell us to not forget when we were older. They were celebrated with cards, affordable gifts in folded wrapping paper or a colorful tissue paper with curling ribbon alongside a home-made cake with candles. The wishes we made were for things like love and success, things others would have guessed. The weather that day would tell us something about ourselves, my January birthday often overcast and gray.

One year when I was in high school, I went downtown to *The James Black Dry Goods Store* which at this point wasn't doing so well with the new mall but was surviving just like me.

Blacks had displayed all of this pop-culture, plastic stuff; bean-bag chairs, blow-up clear plastic chairs, *Coca-Cola* bottles that had been melted and stretched as sculpture, *7-Up* pop cans that had flickering, green-colored light bulbs. The flickering filament image looked like a groovy peace symbol to me. I bought the *Coca-Cola* bottle sculpture and the *7-Up* light for my attic bedroom. I then covered some wood boxes I found in our basement with a navy-blue vinyl.

The first-floor level of *The James Black Department Store* still looked elegant with its high ceilings and its nice department- store, hanging light fixtures. There was a glass-case candy counter in the center with bins of candy like chocolate stars, chocolate malt balls and wonderful chewy orange slices. There was a table display near one entrance with lady's straw bags, the kind with colorful straw flowers. The kind my mom could just afford and would use in Florida at some tropical vacation resort. There was an appliances department on one of the floors with *Sunbeam* products and *Betty Crocker* Cookbooks. The men's department on the main level had a big-city feel to it. And indeed, as I later found out by living and shopping in New York City, it did sort of resemble *Macy's* Men'

Department in its proximity to being just off one corner entrance on the main floor.

Like with every decade, the fads of the time crept down to the masses, to a place like small-town, Waterloo, Iowa. It was what kept us going in a sense, keeping up with the changing times. And there was a lot of heart ache to forget. Deaths and struggles; people living on factory-wage jobs; the Vietnam War.

Plastic *Tupperware* bowls, chiffon shift dresses in paisley prints, bell-bottom jeans. I describe these things because they are what represented us; us being a society that buys lots of consumer products. They offered hope at a time when we needed hope.

It was about this time that things went mod. The British mod subculture had its effects even on small-town Waterloo seen in trickle-down groovy fashions and pop music, mod print dresses, mini-skirts, cool, tight-fitting tailored suits and Beatle records for sale. Then psychedelic music and posters became the thing, shag rugs, Pop art, Op art.

I was now in my early teenage years and this was the rock era of the Beatles. *Lucy in the Sky with Diamonds* played on the radio. It had been on a Beatles album that came out in 1967 a few years previous but still frequently played on the radio. These classic songs were played endlessly on the local Iowa radio stations. I had been raised in a poorer, Christian home and somehow the Beatles and their music were just outside of our spiritual acceptance although I remember seeing them on the *Ed Sullivan Show* on my Grandparents

TV while on a visit to their Northern Missouri farm. I school friend of mine owned most of their records and he proudly showed me this collection in his basement. He had been collecting their records for years and seemed amazed that I knew so little about the group. I neither had the money or the interest really to collect the records. I liked *The Lettermen* and *Herb Albert's Tijuana Brass*, mostly because we had these albums in our meager record collection at home. The Herb Albert album cover, *Whipped Cream & Other Delights*, (the LP was released in 1965) showed a beautiful seated woman with long dark hair holding a long-stemmed rose, naked to our imagination except she was covered in whipped cream to her cleavage. The album colors were an olive green and gold color and the songs listed in a groovy-looking text included, *A Taste of Honey, Tangerine, Love Potion No. 9* and *Lemon Tree*. I played the trumpet in the school band and took lessons from a music teacher at school. I even took lessons from a music teacher at the local college and made some progress in my music technical abilities.

Wide lapel shirts were in and guys had longer hair. Popular girls, cheer-leader types at high school wore their hair long and straight. One girl I remember still cultivated a hippy look. UNI College put on the play, *The Boys in the Band*. The film version of *Godspell* was playing at the Cedar Falls cinema on Main Street. Images of the Vietnam War were on the nightly news. It was endless it seemed this war, the killing, the young men who were losing their lives. And it grew as awful and as sickening as the smell of a burnt, fried-chicken dinner.

There were war protests, "sit-ins" as they were called. Civil-rights marches were covered on the national news. The two-story Victorian houses near UNI campus in Cedar Falls, Iowa had peace symbols and anti-war slogans in their windows. I was only once in one of these college houses; an almost empty living room with a cheap-looking quilt on a bare mattress; a *Steve Miller Band* poster on the wall.

You felt a sense of uneasiness, almost boredom. There seemed to be no escape from the endless Vietnam War, from the conflicts that were emerging. The social conflicts between the young and the old grew worse; between the establishment and the political left; seen in a small town like Waterloo, Iowa mostly on TV.

Soon after I turned sixteen years of age, I found my first job at an establishment that sold men's clothing. A narrow corner store downtown, crowded with men's apparel. The storefront's sign I do not completely remember, but it had the word CLOTHIERS in it. It looked hand painted. The side of the one-story brick building that the store occupied was painted with billboard-type sign. I started work there during the fall. I remember now. It had grown colder outdoors.

The backroom of the men's store was tiny. In it was a steam press, a sewing machine and boxes that lined the walls to the ceiling. Clothing hung on a clothes rack, some finished, some not, threads, manikins, odds and ends. The owner of this establishment was a Jewish man who was also a tailor and he did his tailoring, sewing and streaming in the tiny, crowded room directly behind his storefront retail-store space. Facing the only window in this back room was his sewing machine surrounded by a landscape of boxes that lined the walls. In the center of this room was a large pressing machine that hissed and billowed steam with each crease or press. HIs black-framed glasses would fog over from the steam as he pressed the suspended metal plate into a shirt cuff or sleeve and searched for a pin. He was a small man with baggy slacks pulled high above a short waist. He had the habit of running his finger along the top of his head as if forgetting his hair had receded long ago. His wife was a solidly built woman with dark wavy hair and a fair complexion. She too wore glasses and the attached gold chains dangle on either side of her face as she talked or rang up a sale. She could seem on the verge of anxiety but never really, raising her voice and then giving up on the situation as if to say this is life!

This men's store was only a small, storefront space. It had decent quality suits and sports jackets, dress slacks and men's accessories like hats, socks and suspenders. In the front section of the store were wildly patterned sport shirts, denim bell-bottoms and whatever else the owner hoped would sell. The place was always overstocked and there were leftovers from the past, stacked-up items still in their cardboard boxes', white formal dress shirts with pleated fronts, an out-of-style silk tie, accessories like belts and bowties that had not sold, cuff links, gold, onyx, colored-glass stones in silver-plate. How nicely they glinted in their small velvet boxes. The storefront space would be quiet for a time except for the sound of Joe's pressing or sewing machine then there would be the sudden clang of the front door's bell and the sound of a customer's footsteps across the wood floor.

It was a crowded place in that it lacked space. The floors creaking wood planks.

The ceiling covered with an old-fashioned decorative, patterned tin. The narrow was storefront filled with merchandise. Narrow aisles and the cash register counter crowded with displayed merchandise –men's accessories necessary. The three-way mirror hiding in the hanging sleeve fabric of suits.

It was suiting fabric, silk, felt hats and cotton shifts. The dress shirts crinkled as we took them from their boxes, the shirts covered in new stir, plastic wrapping. Silk ties taken from long boxes coveted as they were put out on display. Stripes and dots, manly diamond patterns and paisleys. In the back of the store the tailoring-stock area was rising steam and clutter.

The owners of the store were Polish and holocaust survivors. They had been forced to leave their home in Poland shortly after the start of World War II. They had children, a daughter and a son. Life was funny in odd ways and it was hard work. The tailor's son came into the store from time to time. He was a bit older than me and with longish, curly hair. The store owner's sister always sat near the front display window of the store each evening starring out at the world with one arm grasping the other. She was white-haired and had a wrinkled face. When she spoke, her face became almost a grimace, her darkly circled eyes lit up with fire. She startled me one evening with the abrupt telling of her time spent in a German concentration camp. She had pulled the baggy sleeve of her red sweater up, showing me the tattooed numbers on her arm and had related this horror casually.

"That's what they did to me," she had said silently by pulling back down the sleeve of her sweater, no longer hiding the ink numbers. She shuffled a bit when she walked, wrapped the open, red sweater around her for extra warmth. Her hands wrinkled, clutching. This woman had found her way but it had been, well, one can only imagine how terrible it must have been. She would then be forgotten, seen later starring out at the world from her storefront window-seat.

How odd the four of us must have looked, me a teenager with my groovy clothes, long blond hair and wire-rim glasses, the Jewish tailor, his wife and his old sister starring out at the world from her window perch. I would learn from my parent's that the young man, my cousin I had been named after, Paul Eugene Bland, had died fighting in France during WW II. He is buried in *Epinal American Cemetery*, Epinal, France. This was my connection to this family.

After a few days, I had learned how to run the cash register, brush the dust off the suits and keep the stacks of clothing neat and orderly. And I learned the proper way to dress the front window. I

81

was instructed on how to pin and tuck the clothing into hidden folds, making a jacket or shirt look perfect and tailored. But as the weather turned cold, the storefront windows frosted over mostly hiding our professional efforts.

The owner would have a customer try on a suit or sports jacket and then block the jacket with his hands, somehow adding to the shape and value of it. Watching with satisfaction as the customer admired himself. Black men patronized the store. They bought tailored bell-bottom slacks, felt hats, silk socks. These had been ordered just for these customers. Groovy, polyester stuff, disco-type shirts with wild, colorful patterns made of acetate, tight-fitting to the body. The stuff sold well and Joe it seemed was always hemming a pair of polyester bellbottoms. So, did the fine, silk socks that he would insist they needed as well.

New shopping malls in Waterloo, Iowa had opened. Downtown merchants left their storefronts empty for a space at the new mall. *Palace Clothiers* was one of these stores. They sold better quality clothing for young men. Displayed one fall in the front section of their new mall store were bell-bottom slacks in sharp, tweedy wools with matching rust or olive-colored print shirts and sweater vests. There were cool-looking belts, soft leather jackets and sports coats in a suede-look material. Waterloo had never seen such cool clothes.

At that age, l was easily influenced. In magazines, I saw men's cool haircuts and handsome manly images, but the reality was that those guys in *GQ* were shopping on Fifth Avenue in New York City.

82

At least that's was it said on the "where to find page" of the magazine Our downtown became the past, vacant and passé. *Black's Department Store* would eventually close. *Osco Drug* stayed open downtown as did the bus station. After a year, I left the Stein's establishment and went to work for *Sears* at the new shopping mall, in the men's department. *Sears* with its new lights and shiny new chrome fixtures. The other guys that worked in the department attended the local college, UNI, (University of Northern Iowa). Cool guys that bragged about their girlfriends and wild partying. Their lives seemed a lot more exciting than mine. My assigned department was men's shirts and ties, a selection of suits and sports jackets, underwear and accessories. Outerwear was in the same department. Corduroy jackets with fleece lining or a thick, down jacket-coat, sufficient for cold Iowa winter. Earth-tone colors were popular, gold, burnt-oranges, olive. Our department was next to the store's exit and I remember the store's outdoor lighting, globes on poles, sometimes barely visible in the middle of a fierce Iowa snow storm. I soon forgot about the Jewish tailor and his small, storefront shop downtown.

Chapter 12

_____

The West side and East side town libraries in Waterloo, Iowa were built with funds donated by Andrew Carnegie. Both classical in architectural style. When I was a young boy, this West Side building was quite imposing and even more so once I passed through the columned entrance and into the quiet of the main room. The year is 1965. It is a Friday evening in spring, perhaps April. The sky threatens rain. I can still remember the smell of fried chicken from supper, the sudsy dish soap that was used to wash the supper dishes; then off to the library. My mother has taken me to the library.

I climb the steps to the columned entrance. Inside the library the hanging glass fixtures glow brightly against the night sky seen outside the tall, large windows. A low voice says, "is due back on…" Someone moves a chair. It makes an abrupt floor-screech noise. Then the upstairs balcony level floor creaks a bit with someone's footsteps.

There's a section of mystery books, current titles, American History. Cooking has a section as well. Children's books are downstairs. I search the upstairs aisles for a book of interest. My tastes are out of the ordinary. Alfred Hitchcock TV stories, ghost stories, a book on UFOs true stories.

I return to the library on another day, this time on my own. The creaking of wood floors and whispering are the only sounds heard besides the slam-crunch noise made by the device that imprinted the blue-ink return date onto the library cards. It seemed like a good day for mystery stories. Black clouds threatened rain and a damp breeze had replaced the late summer heat. The first book I pulled from the shelf was *Hound of the Baskervilles*. It was a worn copy with a very British Holmes on the cover and a misty scene in the background. There were a whole section of Sherlock Holmes books and I examined each one. The covers were all eerie settings with Holmes and Watson in the process of investigation. I continued my search. The room was noticeably darker now and a gray-black sky covered the tall library windows.

Next to the Library was the *Grout Museum* with exhibits on the history of Waterloo that told visitors Pioneer stories. There were recreated settings of early American rooms, antique bicycles and a set of very large gemstones that told us about rocks and minerals. There was a planetarium as well. I went there with a friend from school and we saw the afternoon show on the galaxy. The lights dimmed and a black cutout skyline of our town, Waterloo appeared backlit by an artificial horizon and then the stars appeared in the sky, so real you could swear you were outside at night. It was amazing. In the center of the room was the machine that projected the tiny pins of light toward the ceiling. This metal ball glowed with pins of light and rotated as the man who gave us the demonstration on the solar system guided us through time and the shifting of the sky's position.

He pointed out constellations and far away planets. He spoke of great distances and light years. In junior high I belonged to astronomy club and we went one evening to a small observatory at one of the newer high schools. We climbed the stairs to the top level. Inside the observatory was a telescope underneath a metal dome with an opening. There were no lights inside and we used a flashlight to find our position with the telescope. Our plan was to find the planet Saturn with its rings and this we did, barely visible in the telescope but there it was. Outside was the grassy land adjacent to the school's parking lot. The star-filled sky was not as dark as in the country. The surrounding neighborhood, a newly built, upscale addition of homes lit up with electric lights.

1990s

My reason for walking downtown was to purchase a newspaper and I needed to get out of the house. I had reached the raised highway that now cut through the edge of downtown. A block away and up the hill was the *Grout Museum*.

At the corner, another block away was the original *Waterloo Public Library*. I had spent many evenings wandering through the short aisles of this library. The building that had built with Carnegie's money now looked surprisingly small, a limestone box that defied its new owners, a group of attorneys, by still looking like a library. I had been to this place on many after-dinner evenings with my mother. The dishes done, the leftover food now put away.

I purchased my newspaper at the *National Cigar Store* on the East side of Waterloo. I had then crossed the bridge back to the West side of the *Cedar River* and had continued walking back home, past the rows of two-story wood houses. Blocks of houses that looked pretty much the same. I finally reached our rough, tar-covered street with its houses that did not match in style or size. I found my father in a chair angled toward a dark television. My mother was in her room resting after more chemotherapy. He rose from his chair slowly, as if offered no other choice. He paused for a moment after standing and then walked out the side door into the yard. I sat in the same chair, and began to read my newspaper. A few minutes later, I set aside the newspaper and then approached the door of my mother's room. It was slightly open and I could see that she was still awake and seemed to be reading a book. I then backed away from the door and left her undisturbed.

My mother passed away that late November. She had overcome her self-doubts years before and she had gone on to college and she had earned a college degree. Then, she had worked as a home health-care aid for many years. She was dearly loved by many people. The flowers and plants sent at the time of the funeral didn't seem enough as they probably never do for a loved one. She was a terrific lady.

Those months home were the first I had spent in Waterloo, Iowa as an adult. I had never really been very close to my father and now the two of us were living in his house together and the silence between us was deafening. A sister of mine would come by and clean the rooms of the tiny house, tearing-up while she wiped or scrubbed things whistle clean having found some reminder of our mother. This older sister of mine, only eleven months older than myself, had moved back home to Iowa.

My father and I never ate a meal together and when he did eat he sat at the table staring out grimly, at the past perhaps but he seemed to have moved on already and he kept busy with his small improvements to the house as he had decided to sell.

It was the world that my mother had willed to me; the world and books. I began to read to escape the dreadful emptiness of our house. Books from the library, Chekhov and Henry James, F. Scott Fitzgerald and Isaac Singer. In the next few years I would begin to write as well; short stories and a few poems that I would put away. It was an accomplishment. My first stories I titled, *My Waterloo.*

I wandered into a downtown bar, not for alcohol but to experience the place. Less-fortunate locals in booths, caught-up in their small-town lives, were telling each other loud, insistent stories, important dramas, expressing injustices, outrages, this between swills of liquor. There were beer posters on the wall, a reflection of the bar's neon sign in the behind-the-bar mirror. A jukebox cranks up and begins to play a country-western song and right then and there, I remembered that I had been living on the California West Coast. Boy, was I from out-of-town.

The Library 2001-2003

The current Waterloo Public Library resides in the old city hall building, newly renovated with a computer section and lounge seating. There are tables and chairs along the windows upstairs. There is a section for DVDs and CDs, new titles and express books.

If you are in a library for any real length of time it starts to appear a bit grungy. It is a public space after all, a high-use public space. Things wear out quickly. Things get smudged, dirty, stolen. It depends on the library of course. I've been in the Beverly Hills Public Library and I wouldn't call it grungy. The Rodin sculptures help. The Chicago Library has lots of space. Here there are lots of places to take a book to read. That's nice. The Waterloo Library is only slightly grungy. It is nicely furnished and for the most part clean. The staff is nice. They have great used book sales. I wouldn't say I have great memories of this place, but I did find some interesting books. And in a small town with not a lot to do it was a valued destination.

Chapter 13

It is a summer morning. I look outdoors through a window at our backyard. It is already warm and sunny and the grass in the yard is a bright, rich green. It is a day for travel in campers to vacation lakes and wooded parks. It is a day for common garden flowers, bees and the ordinary sounds of any small-town neighborhood. It is a day for sticky, dripping *Orange-sicle* pops and the public swimming pool. A breeze moves the branches of the elm tree in our backyard but only slightly. On summer days like this we might have a bacon, lettuce and tomato sandwich on white bread with mayo. We might talk about an errand and put it off, like a trip to the grocery store or drug store. It is the main event of the day, our only commercial venture. The television set plays soap-operas we turn off. We are devoid of music, something you hear on a car radio or at church on a Sunday morning.

I learned about the world mostly through school, my parents, church and television, television sitcoms and consumer product commercials that kept me entertained and occupied. I remember my father each evening consuming his dinner and the six o'clock news, editorializing between bites of food. My parents never bought magazines and only occasionally bought our town newspaper, *The*

Waterloo Daily Courier. I read very few books outside of school and comic books and movie-theater movies were forbidden. Although, I remember sneaking out to the movie theater downtown with a boyhood friend. The film was a B-western full of cowboys and savage Indians. *Buzzby Wing Drug* was the only commercial establishment within walking distance of our house besides the corner grocery. The drug store had a soda fountain counter. It sold medicines, greeting cards and stationary supplies, candy and small gifts for birthdays.

The cool days of spring and blooming flowers were now just a memory. The soggy, rain-soaked earth of April had dried and a warm breeze shook the dark green leaves of trees. A clear blue sky appeared almost daily. It became increasingly warmer and the weeds and wildflowers grew abundantly in the field behind our house. I was too young to hold a salaried job and so I mowed a lawn, raked leaves or worked in an old person's garden to earn money. My father might tell me about these yard jobs.

Our downtown still thrived somewhat but rumors of a new mall just South of town meant that most of its businesses would close or relocate within a few years. One corner entrance of *Black's Department Store*, its main street level, was the entrance to its men's shop. Now it sold Bermuda shorts and pullovers, cotton sweaters for rich doctors who golfed on weekends. Colorful short-sleeved sport shirts hung on a circular rack. Even men's cologne was on sale next to handkerchiefs and cufflinks. But it was all too expensive for me and I walked through the racks with indifference -but often, as I loved to look at all this big-city, retail merchandise.

The orange lilies along the fence were wet with morning dew that dried quickly in the burning sun. There was the sound of a lawn mower at a distance, no promise of rain in the clear sky. Even the white clouds offered no response. It was a day for drifting they told you.

"I'm going to have to get your dad to fix the railing on the patio," my mother might say coming outside from the side door of the house, a task that required the pouring of concrete to patch a hole where the railing was once secured.

"I'm going to have some ice tea with lemon and enjoy this weather. Paul, would you like some ice tea?" asked my mother.

"Sure," I might have said. But we had no lemon and the neighborhood corner grocery certainly didn't have one. Good thing the ice-tea was lemon flavored already and sweetened with *Sweet and Low*. It grew hotter as mid-day approached. Gnats were visible above the weeds and grass in the field behind the house. I burned easily in the sun and did not know how to swim. The pool at *Byrnes Park* was out of the question.

It did rain that summer, the day growing cooler and darker by the minute. It was late morning and then the rain came; thunder, lighting and a sudden, hard rain that would help the crops of corn grow quickly. I was upstairs in my attic room with the window open, letting the rain splash a bit on my face as I looked out. First there was the flash of lighting seen in the distance and then a second or two later the thunder, crashing loud. Rain swelled at the edges of our tar street. I thought of the cupcakes I had seen at the school's ice-cream social for some reason. A robin flew onto the shingled roof of our house and shook itself then took off for a tree branch. Lightings flashed in the distance. I was glad for the rain. It gave me a reason to reflect.

The August humidity was almost intolerable and now we longed for fall. It rained again on an overcast day and it bored us for it changed nothing. Dinner was left-over fried chicken and the rest of a potato salad that we had been served for Sunday after-church dinner. It was time for an adventure, but nothing came to mind. Money was scarce and we only had our imaginations although we wouldn't have admitted it.

Even with a slight breeze it was stifling hot that summer day. The leaves of the giant cotton wood tree showed off their whitish undersides. The leaves on the lilac tree in our back yard slightly wilted and brown in places. The purple flowers of lilacs only a memory.

That summer in Iowa was as uneventful as all the previous summers had been. It would be breezy and warm some days and insufferably hot and humid on others. Flowers bloomed in our yard and in the yard of the Manning's behind our house. This is where I discovered the magazines that would occupy a good portion of my time on those summer days, in the garage and basement of the Manning's house.

It was the summer before I entered high school. One afternoon I was crossing through Mrs. M's garden. She had an amazing garden with rows and rows of flowers in perfectly neat beds. She said hello from the back door of their house. She was a stout lady, usually wearing stretch slacks and a full silky blouse. I was led to a room downstairs where we found stacks of magazines.

"You are welcome to these. We have way too many," she stated.

"Now have you ever seen a magazine like that? She asked offering me a copy of *Ebony*. What do you think of that?" I looked inside and found one or two white people in ads for consumer products only. I didn't respond as I do not think I knew what to say.

Mr. Manning as it turned out worked for the Courier, our town newspaper and the Manning couple seemed to read a lot of different publications. There were stacks, glossy, topical, literary, copies of *Life, National Geographic, The New Yorker,* and *Ebony.*

That summer was uneventful, hot and humid. We seemed poor as usual, but it was summer after all, no school and there were a few events to mark the calendar. A visit from relatives the reason for a picnic, the Fourth of July, watermelon, extra money earned from yard work and those magazines given to me by Mrs. Manning. How sophisticated I had suddenly become in my attic room, articles and glossy ads, funny New Yorker cartoons, editorials and short stories I didn't read.

Chapter 14

———————

Mostly during the summer months, we would visit relatives in Missouri.

The Northern Missouri land was hilly and wooded. A place of woods and rocky ledges. Of hills, rivers and streams. Tilled were the level and fertile sections of land for planting. The country roads led to pleasant-looking small towns. The kind of town where you might raise a family. Within the structures were the architectural elements of many styles. But American was the best way to describe most of the structures in these small towns. Basic two-story wood homes with porches and brick storefronts on a main street. Buildings built from local lumber and stone. Missouri towns influenced by a southern sensibility, that was more apparent in the lower part of the state. It could be a lazy place of heat and humidity or one of activity, conscious of commerce and the need to prosper and compete. An education and common sense evident in the outcome of achievement.

In rural Putnam County, the summer heat and rain caused the grass and thickets to grow quickly. Bugs filled the air along with moths and butterflies that fluttered above flowering weeds and the tall field grass. It was the summer that seemed to make this place come alive. The sounds of animals and birds heard in the trees. Deer alongside the road. Evening came like a relief. The cooler air and the dusk. And the Missouri night sky above filled with the constellation of stars and a visible milky way. It caused you to wonder about life and the meaning of it. It could be romantic, or a great mystery never solved.

The rural road at night was never a certainty. A fog, rainstorm or a heavy snow could leave it unpassable or unseen. In normal weather, your car's headlights directed you along its gravel way. The surrounding woods and fields only darkness.

You never forgot this place. Its night views that were limited to the sky and the darkened land around you. The intense heat of summer and when snow left the hills and woods half-white. Fallen trees and thicket like a mantle rising to a plain, gray sky. Small gardens near farm houses and the houses in town with flowers and vegetables like roses, orange-lilies; root and fruit vegetables. Life was simple here and when you left this place you realized it without saying so. As if civilization had again commenced in all its pace and modernity.

Each spring came with its new green and bright blue sky. Summer with its warm breeze and the cooling taste of well water in a tin cup. The land here held places to be discovered like a stream in the woods or a rock ledge at the edge of a hillside. Its shadows never allowing a full view of all land levels and shapes. In that way, it always seemed to hold a mystery and so it was romantic too, as it was never fully revealed or told. Like a story without a final ending.

It was one of those hot, summer days when stopping for a rest from the tar heat and a sticky, vinyl car seat is no longer a choice. I was thirteen years of age that summer and walking down the Main Street of a small Northern Missouri town carrying a can of soda pop that had tumbled from the gas station's soda-pop vending machine. This at the same gas station and general store where my father was now checking the oil of our overheated Ford Galaxy and filling its tank with gas. My mother was wearing her new vacation sunglasses and making a phone call to an old family friend from the pay phone while fanning herself with a map of the Midwest. These Northern Missouri towns were towns with town squares, neat brick storefronts and friendly home-cooked meal restaurants. The men in town wore starched, white short-sleeved shirts and slacks or a pair of overalls. The ladies wore cotton print dresses and sometimes a hat.

Pool Room the sign said revealing what was behind a ground floor row of screened windows that belonged to a corner storefront. I looked inside through the screen door. Through a haze of metal-mesh I could see a green, felt-covered pool table. The place was completely empty of life. I turned and walked back in the blazing sun and stifling humidity, back to the gas station and back inside the gas station-store, cool and dark, barely lit by sparse, yellowed fluorescent lighting that flickered a bit at the edges. The general store offered cold soft drinks (mine consumed) and maps, necessities like flexible combs and *Pepto-Bismol*, candy bars and canned food, farm supplies, too many things to notice or remember. A calendar on the wall advertised *Coca-Cola.* The sound of the bell on the entrance screen door rang as it opened, outside the screen door was the sound of gravel under a slow car's tires and seen, a cloud of dust. The man in the store, his Missouri drawl not sounding quite southern, gave road directions to my father. We soon reached the highway where we had turned off, leaving the noise of the gravel from under our tires and passing the same highway truck stop with its 'Good Food and Gas' sign.

We stopped again along our rural Missouri route, this time to visit a relative before heading on to the Henricks in another Missouri town. The relative's yard was over-grown with grass, the farm house only whitewashed with paint. There was a water-well. Soup was still on the stove in the kitchen with its big, open cupboards and worn linoleum floor. There was old-fashioned, mohair furniture in the front room, photographs of unrecognized, ghost-like relatives in oval frames. This is what I remember of this farm place along with the orange lilies than grew alongside the house.

We gave a look, out back towards the surrounding land. The relative mentions the years of clutter on the back porch. A reassurance of love and were on our way again down the winding, gravel road past hilly pasture and wooded areas between the plowed farmland. If you travel at night in this part of Missouri, the sound of gravel under car tires becomes louder, as loud as the crickets and above you a pitch-black, star-filled sky.

Mrs. Henrick wore a summery, sleeveless dress cinched at the waist with a little thin belt and with a square, low neckline that showed her ample bosom.

The Henricks had a newer house, ranch-style and the inside walls of the house were smooth, freshly painted sheetrock. Their living room was modern. A boat-shaped, glass candy dish sat on the coffee table. An orange zigzag-patterned blanket partially covered the back section of a new sofa.

My parents loved the Henrick's new home. They could only dream of such luxury! In young Kyle Henrick's room, he kept his collection of *Elvis Presley* records and baseball cards, a few model racecars (half finished), sports equipment, college pennants and priceless, one-of-a kind memorabilia.

We drove to *Lake Thunderhead*. A view of it shiny and blue between the trees. The inside of our car smelled of *Coppertone* lotion and the stuffy heat was now barely tolerable with only a lagging warm breeze from the car's open windows.

You could see the lake clearly now as the road descended closer to the shore. A line of water foam on the lake trailed behind a motorboat barely heard and a few bathers were waist deep in the lake water near a boat dock and a mud and sand slip of beach. There were picnic tables on a grassy patch of land that tilted towards the lake, not very shaded and so we drove on.

"That's a pretty spot" said my mother, pointing in the direction of a shady ground under a group of trees but my father drove on much to her annoyance. He wanted to find a place to park that was nearer the boat docks.

"Don't get so excited!" said my father practically, as we escaped the stuffy, sticky heat of the parked car.

The lakebed was muddy and mossy but the water clear and cool. I could see schools of tiny fish like a flash of copper just below the water's surface. I took off my shoes and socks, rolled up my jeans and then waded into the cool water stirring up clouds of mud oozing up under my bare feet.

When I was a young teenager, my father bought a farm in this place, this area of Northern Missouri. A typical two-story farmhouse painted white along with eighty acres of land adjacent to the farmhouse and yard. It had belonged to my great-grandmother.

The most memorable thing about this house was that it had two wood-varnished columns that flanked an opening from one first floor room into another. It gave a kind of grandeur to the house. The old house was not unusual in any other aspect really.

I remember that I was assigned the task of wallpapering the upstairs rooms of the house, small bedrooms with slanted ceilings. The wallpaper bought at a discount. The sticky wallpaper paste created a mess, until the wallpaper was hung and smoothed out onto the wall. There were bubbles to resolve and mismatched seams. The small rooms transformed with repeated patterns of tiny flowers or Americana scenes of flags and drums.

There were photographs attached to this house, of our great

101

grandmother, of my brother and sisters and of relatives we didn't know or recognize, at first. The backyard of this farmhouse was overgrown with tall grass and weeds. There were Plum trees. My father would sell the place a few years later. An aunt and uncle lived nearby. Their small farmhouse was set in a low, wooded area of land just off a gravel road. The woods edged the yard of this house with its encircling, ground-level porch. At night, the light from the windows of the house barely lit the yard and so you never ventured too far, from adult voices telling stories; reminiscing. In a room where my cousins slept, I was shown items taken from a dresser drawer. My cousins kept stuff in cigar boxes, mineral rocks, souvenirs, and ribbons from the county fair. I remember visiting their schoolhouse. It was a one-room schoolhouse and I remember seeing a play they put on there. A tinfoil moon rising above a backdrop curtain of sheeting material and a minimal stage set. The words I don't remember.

It was a quiet, black Missouri night, quiet except for the sound of crickets and insistent moths that fluttered against a bare light bulb that lit up the screen door area of the wood porch. This front porch framed my aunt and uncle's farmhouse. Fireflies were visible in the low-lying yard that sloped downwards towards the thick, wooded area that edged the farmyard and pasture land of the farm. Light from the windows of the house dimly lit up the porch and the voices of my parents and my aunt and uncle could be heard from indoors. It was a place of rusty cold well water, potato soup and homemade bread spread with churned butter. My cousins both boys and girls all had hair of corn silk, too long and cut by my uncle. We would visit and then leave. We were city folk, back to my grandmother's house or onto Kirksville to visit another relative.

I remember summer family reunions in Northern Missouri at the one-room school house in this rural area. A creaking wood floor, metal pans of food, cakes and pies, paper plates, like a church pot luck supper. The hot Missouri sun shined down on the yard of the schoolhouse creating narrow shadows on the whitewashed building. There were other summer vacations to places like the Black Hills or even as far as Denver, Colorado. But our visits to Missouri were the most memorable.

Chapter 15

_____

As I grew older I continued to attend church with my family but at times I resented the fervent reaction of the congregants and their urging of others to renew their faith or ask forgiveness of sins. This occurred often during an evening service when the preacher might call on congregants to come forward and repent as in a bible revival service. Members of the church would give testimony about their own salvation and urge others to repent of sin or remember God's blessing. Somehow, I seemed outside of it and yet I knew I believed in something. I didn't really know what an atheist was and I have never been one. But as an adolescent I silently rejected the spiritual drama I observed by others. I was separate from the outstanding Christians that lead the singing or helped pass the offering plate. It was a feeling that would cause me to push away any spiritual thought as a young adult. The spiritual was tied only to these Christians who under great conviction had called me a sinner.

I am watching television in my attic room on my small black and white television. It is snowing in Waterloo, Iowa. It is nightfall and slushy outdoors and snowing. I am a teenager. I have long hair and wear long-sleeve knit tops in burgundy stripes or browns. My wire-rimmed glasses are gold. I have discovered sex and alcohol and hear rumors of classmates using drugs. Life is trippy, faith in God, sinful, joyful and marked with holidays and Sunday mornings at church. All of this will pass away within a decade or two. I just do not know it or care to know it. I am unique and special because my mother tells me so and my girlfriend. I feel connected to the changing weather and seasons in ways that I am not sure others do as well. If I am a poet I do not know it. I am sensitive and evidently girlish at times. But I walk carefully now. I remain quiet and observing. I have learned to survive who I am and that is someone I am getting to know. I am defiant when I acknowledge and aspect of myself. I am young and bright.

In the early 1970's downtown Waterloo, Iowa was re-planned and renovated. The old theater was torn down. A new convention center was built and a river bridge with a covered walkway. The art deco styled *YMCA* building was renovated as well and divided into offices. The dime stores and *J.C. Penny* went the way of the wrecking ball, as they say. The downtown *J.C. Penney's* building was demolished November, 1979.

People graduated from high school, handsome guys with longish-hair, and girls as pretty as ever. Couples that were in love and that would soon be married.

I was working downtown at the Jewish tailor's but would soon be employed at the mall, at *Sears*'s men's department. I was a good salesman by now.

Some of the older wood houses in town took on renovations.

New doors that didn't match the rest of the old wood house, new porches attached, yard crafts, aluminum siding. The houses in Waterloo represented individuals. Their lawns and the type of house they occupied and the materials that the house was made of. One newly renovated house on Third Avenue was covered in a wood-shingle siding and the trim of the house was now an olive green. They celebrated with orange-colored mum plants on their front steps. I was a teenager now, and I would often walk home from high school past these neighborhood houses. I would be an adult soon and maybe have my own house and yard someday. The possibility seemed remote, but at that age you feel that anything is possible. That is your state of mind. And you are invincible physically. People from our church congregation passed away and you were reminded of immortality. It made things seem less real and yet more so, like shadows.

People traded their younger looks for more practical clothing, graying hair, loss; slow acceptance of change. Nostalgia could be found in things like antiques or storytelling of the past.

In the seventies, I would begin to collect American art pottery. My mother began to collect this as well. It was something that we had in common although we lived in great distance apart from each other. In her endless search, a few good pieces were found, very few though, as collecting American art pottery seemed to be growing in popularity. It was sweet of her to want to share this with me and she enjoyed searching for pottery at local garage sales. These were mostly pieces with USA or *McCoy* or *Red Wing* on the bottom of the pot, lots of depression greens, turquoise, aqua, speckled pink, cream or perhaps a bright yellow. Pots that were sometimes cracked or chipped, glazes shiny or matted, pots in odd shapes and ugly colors like army green that no one would want. Pottery I would find like treasures in our basement upon returning home. As she lay dying in her room of cancer, it is what I did. Endlessly search through the countless pieces of art pottery she had collected over the years, stashed away in plastic bins and boxes. It got me through it, frankly, an awful time. And then I had the realization that she had done this as well, when she needed to escape in a sense. And like books it was something we could share.

There was her last hope in getting well, our last talk together (when she seemed well enough), the last hug, the last gift and the last goodbye. While she was sick she was angry, uncomplaining, forgiving, spiritual (she sang church hymns) and unselfish. She loved books, learning, life, sharing and caring for others. Right before she passed away I looked at her hands, so alive and perfect. The time was evening and I went outside and looked up at the moon in the sky, mottled and shiny.

Chapter 16

I rode with my father to work so we could have use of the car. Each morning I went downstairs and sat near the table while my father finished his breakfast. The room was almost dark except for a light above the kitchen sink. His back was to me and he starred ahead as if I had not entered the room. Neither of us spoke and the only signal that it was time to go was when he walked out the door of the house and the starting of the car's engine.

This morning, he flipped through the car's radio channels looking for some acceptable sound to break our silence. He settled on a station that must have seemed tolerable to him -just tolerable enough perhaps like his average day at the meat packing plant. He remained silent with me. I was still afraid of him at times, but it wasn't a painful silence between us. I would be leaving for college soon and I knew he cared about me. He was a good man, a good father despite his terrible arguments with my mother.

He walked away from the car that morning without emotion as he always did. I noticed him more this morning and I watched him as he walked huddled against the cold wind with his lunch pail towards the large, ugly brick packing-plant. How bleak the town of Waterloo seemed that morning as I drove back home past the row of *Rath*'s smoke stacks and across a noisy, rattling, 'erector-set' bridge.

I helped with a garden that summer, for an older woman, wealthier, bright. The brick one-story house was in that better area of town, on the hilly edge of our more modest neighborhood. She had a garden room, a porch with comfortable wicker furniture fitted with floral patterned cushions and leafy plants. An old-fashioned telephone sat on a small bamboo end table. She was practical and firm, fair, and her manner equaled simple intelligence.

"Pull that small weed by the roots. Get rid of that crab grass."

People with money in Waterloo seemed very practical. They might improve a house or sod a lawn, but they got a good price. People took pride in their homes. I knew this because I did yard work and odd jobs for them. A more upscale neighborhood edged ours. A garage was organized, things in their place for annual retrieval such as a garden hose, rake, the storm or screen windows.

Chapter 17

The same seventies pop music played on the local radio station incessantly, as it must have in all small towns USA, like ours. You thought of that. How the music reflected the time. Songs with lyrics you had tired of long ago.

Clothes changed. People died or were born. Downtown stores closed that wouldn't re-open. Hobby shops, second-hand bookstores. A relative would appear and give us important news of more relatives I didn't know. Important news they insisted silently. A season milder or the same; or was it? The place got older too.

One of the few spontaneous things I ever remember my father doing was buying me a car. It was a '62 *Buick Skylark* convertible. It ran well and the top worked.

The elm tree in our backyard was cut down. A victim of Dutch Elm disease. It marked another time. Clothing styles changed and people got older. Many downtown Waterloo stores closed that wouldn't re-open. A relative would appear and give us important news of more relatives I didn't know. A season milder or the same - or was it? The place got older too.

I had grown taller than my father but only slightly. My mother was decidedly short and she told me with pride how tall and broad-shouldered I had grown. I was to finish high school that next year. I held a job and a driver's license to drive a car. The town had grown smaller in size to me. The Wesleyan church easily found. A trip to the shopping mall on the Southern edge of town a chance to listen to the pop song hits on the car radio. From the highway on the way to the mall was the sight of corn fields and the new hospital where people went to die or live on.

I had grown taller than my father but only slightly. My mother was decidedly short and she told me with pride how tall and broad-shouldered I had grown. I was to finish high school that next year. I held a job and a driver's license to drive a car.

I was still attached to downtown as it was a reminder of the past, my growing up, my lone trips downtown on the bus. To me it represented the big city only a smaller version with proper retail stores and restaurants. The light and shadow on the brick buildings, the gleam of big-city diners and traffic, neon signs that beckoned you to have a cocktail. It was freedom to me. A place to choose what I wanted even at a young age. like the times I went there with money to buy something for a member of my family or myself. The basket of flowers pin for my mother. That cowboy shirt at *Wards* I wanted so badly and received. But it wasn't just a place to buy things. It was a place to discover as well. There was a mystery around ever brick corner even if it were never really solved.

I am writing this book. While writing one day, I made notes in a tablet:

Byrnes Park -the twisted trunks of the silver maple trees, a

111

towering sugar maple with smooth, gray branches.

Byrnes Park golf course was on the edge of the best residential area of town. Prospect Boulevard. We lived on the edge of this residential area of town as well but the difference in real estate value plunged dramatically after Home Park Boulevard.

I wandered up to the golf clubhouse one sunny summer day. There was a rose garden nearby and a pro-shop. On the corner near the clubhouse, just up the hill and past the rose garden was a very nice, Tudor-style house. In the wide, shaded driveway was parked a foreign sports car, a little red *GM* or *Ferrari*. I imagined myself living there as the rich son of some good-looking, well-bred couple. All I had to do was drive around in my sports car, play a little golf, and then have dinner with a girlfriend who was wild for me. I then would pack my luggage for another tedious trip to Europe. I had even found the car l might drive in a used car lot not far from where we really lived. A small car lot near *Clute's Grocery*, overgrown with sedge grass, the car lot office windows boarded up. The car was an *Alfa Romeo* convertible-a bit rusted but an early sixties classic with chrome detailing and an all-leather interior. With a little fixing up it would be perfect.

I have one brother. I have two sisters. I love them very much and I realize the importance of our relationships. Our father was always exhausted from work at the packing plant. And so it seemed I had no choice but to be closest to my mother. She was my best friend. And it was the same for her too, especially when I was younger. We escaped to the public library together. We watched old movies on television late at night, planned holidays and shared moments of spontaneous laughter or joy suddenly produced like the string of colorful, glowing plastic patio lights hung out on a tree in our back yard', sipping ice-tea in new lawn chairs and listening to our own hushed voices against the sounds of an Iowa summer night. She had given me two books when I was very young. One on world religions and the other was a book on film movie stars. I loved them both. The only other book on our few bookshelves that I remember was *The Pearl*, by Ernest Hemingway. This and several thin encyclopedias bought on sale from the local grocery store. And that was it.

It is the 1980s and we are having a family picnic lunch after our appointment at the photo studio. This being one of those portrait studios in a small town anyone would recognize, with the big glossy wedding portrait in the window, portraits of adorable kids and remarkably good-looking high-school graduates.

We unpacked our picnic lunch at *Byrnes Park*. But as we sat there together having this picnic lunch, to me, the others in my family were missing the moment. In a sense, I was there alone. Not when our heads were bowed in prayer before our meal -but afterward. l hadn't closed my eyes you see. I rarely did this during a prayer. For some reason. It wasn't self-importance l felt but an importance for living and sharing, of not noticing the petunias and miniature marigolds planted in clever patterns in the park. We lived in one of those better brick houses across the street from the park. At least we should have. They were special to me and despite all of our faults and arguments we were so very typically American and good and our family more important than the life circumstances that would soon take us in different directions. We're here together I said to myself -perhaps for the last time. And as it turned out I was right. The family portrait had been taken. We looked very nice together. We had enjoyed each other's company, my parents so pleased by the moment, the grass and flowers in the park, potato salad and lemonade. The old plaid cooler never found. There is a spoken memory of a favorite aunt or uncle. The quiet between us said the rest.

There were the times my parents drove me to the train station in Dubuque to return to New York City. My first trip to this train station along the Mississippi River was on a bus and I slept on a train bench the night before the train arrived in the early morning hours. It had become a part of my trips home to Waterloo. This connection of small town Iowa and New York City was an odd one, uncomfortable for me at times and I am sure my family as well. And returning home was, well, jarring at times. I had grown accustomed to my life in the big city. Things were slower here and you worked hard, saw to the crops, the growing children and whatever business was at hand.

There was time for the *Iowa State Fair* and weekends at *Okabogee Lake*.

During my visits home, one of the small bedrooms in our house was given to me. My mother had placed bits and pieces of my adolescence there; little gifts left behind, like a book I had given my mother on a birthday. In this room, there was a chilly breeze from the backyard window in the mornings. The bed covered with too many blankets and a starchy bedspread. The closet and dresser filled, resigning my suitcase to a corner of the room. The memory of New York City living mixed with the sight of Iowa fields and farm buildings.

Chapter 18

The remaining cake on my father's March sixth birthday cake was put back in its pink cardboard box, white cake with sugary icing from *Johnson's Bakery*.

My father's wish was to drive out to Airline Highway and to the airport, on the way stopping for ice cream. Airline highway had two distinctive landmarks, a *Tastee Freeze* and a miniature golf course. The miniature golf course a tiny town of brightly painted buildings on astro turf, lit by glaring white lights that left you feeling as though you were missing the fun if you passed by without stopping. I had been to the airport once previously on a balmy summer night, a flat rectangular building with waterloo Municipal Airport' in precise chrome letters above its glass and steel-framed entrance. Inside were rows of molded plastic chairs, a metal carousel for luggage and vending machines. As you approached the building and runways from the highway you could see flashing red and blue lights on tall antennae in the distance rising above the observation deck and tower.

Standing at the edge of the observation deck, my father pointed out an in-coming plane gleaming silver against the blue sky as it descended towards the lights that outlined the runway. My mother began to tell a story. My father found the story too silly to tolerate. Now she quietly looked out at the runway and adjusted the nylon scarf tied around her dark, reddish hair with angry hands. She spoke again but this time sounding defensive and my father responded with a voice not wholly apologetic and with satisfaction at having taken command of her emotions. A plane now taxied off the runway as a man gave directions with hand-held illuminated bars of light that flashed bright orange. A voice from a microphone called out a jumble of words and numbers as the three of us walked down the metal stairwell that echoed our footsteps against cement walls and back to our car.

This highway part of town, on the edge of town would always bring back an odd collection of memories. The miniature golf course with its tiny village of buildings lit up in floodlights', the vanilla ice cream cones with red candy cherries at the highway *Dairy Queen*. And the highway near the rural house and yard of the elderly church couple that came to visit my mother and read the bible with fervor.

It is 1973. I put on a pair of gray bellbottom slacks. These look like denim but are of a thinner material. They have white stitching which looks cool. With these I wear an olive-green shirt. I look in the mirror above my old dresser and comb my long blond hair that is parted on one side and curls in the back.

It was just another school night. Mom and dad are arguing again. We are broke, always broke and I am not ok. Different that is for sure and not the best student but the best just the same because I like music and notice things like flowers and the color of the grass in spring. I would never mention this to others as I am not completely aware of it myself. I am just different and loved.

When I was seventeen, I went off to Paris as a summer exchange student. It was a long summer visit of more than three months. This was my next experience with the airport, a return flight from Chicago at age seventeen. I was returning from Europe on a connecting flight from Chicago. How neat the airport looked from above; flat-roofed rectangles and rows of angled parked cars, disrupting the perfect order only with their different shades of color.

Two sisters from our church made me a sports jacket to wear that summer, made of a light blue cotton fabric. The jacket had white stitching and blue buttons. It looked great with my white bucks. These two sisters were the sweetest things. They had taken on a hippy style of dressing. I remember the groovy curtain of beads that hung between the rooms in the first floor of their old house and the wild, paisley smock tops they had made for themselves. Their parents never seemed to be around. I was only seventeen and I had never traveled farther than say the gulf coast of Texas or Florida with my parents. Before I went off to Paris, friends from high school gave me a surprise "going away" party. Only once before had I been given a surprise party, this on a birthday when I was in elementary school. My reaction was embarrassment mostly and then a smiling acknowledgement of the gesture. I was quiet and reserved growing up and although I deeply appreciated this gesture, I did not know how to react to it. I was a keen observer. But at school I usually tried my best to not be noticed, too much. I played an instrument, the coronet, in the school orchestra and jazz band. I had joined Chorus and drama club. (I played the bit part of the magistrate in, *A School for Husbands.*) I absolutely loved Chorus and I have a good voice like my mother. Never was I happier than when we performed choral music on stage or when I participated in a program of music with the school orchestra or band.

On the way to Paris, at an airport shop, I bought a copy of William Burrough's, *The Naked Lunch.* I thought it was sexy filth at the time.

After returning to Waterloo as an older adult, I remember leaving Waterloo airport once. My flight was the first one out that morning. I was left at the entrance at my insistence not wanting to delay the goodbye to my father, reasoning that he needn't spend money on an airport parking fee. It was that awkward, sad moment we have all experienced. He then left abruptly, and I carried my suitcase into the bright fluorescent light of the small terminal and sat in one of the rows of plastic molded seats.

Chapter 19

_____

One year while living in Los Angeles, I decided to return home for Christmas. I had scheduled a flight to Chicago *O'Hara* airport where I would have a layover and then catch a flight home to Waterloo, Iowa. The plane that was to take us there was a small propeller plane. The passengers had boarded and we had waited to leave but a snow storm had quickly turned into a blizzard and after waiting a very long time inside the plane, it finally began to taxi on the runway.

"We're going to try and make it," the stewardess had told the passengers. We were terrified; at least I know I was. Then the plane came to a sudden stop before it even took off. Then there was the announcement that the flight had been cancelled. We then exited the plane and returned to the airport lounge. It was decided that the passengers would be taken to Iowa on buses. We transferred our luggage and boarded the *Greyhound* buses.

The bus was filling up with servicemen and women in uniform and with some of us from the stranded plane that was to fly us to Iowa. The bus finally left the airport and soon we were on the road. It was snowing hard and visibility was surprisingly limited. We passed small-town commercial areas along the highway that were a blur of neon signs and blowing snow, barely visible gas stations or highway restaurants then the open, almost indistinguishable view of fields, valleys and trees. I was tired, and my body ached from the trip home on first a plane from Los Angeles and then this unexpected ride home to Iowa on a *Greyhound* bus. Christmas packages were visible above the seats in the bus. Quickly wrapped packages in dime-store wrapping or brown paper tied with twine. The bright Christmas lights of yet another Christmas tree flashed past us as we continued West towards Iowa.

One small-town bus station had decorated their window with Christmas lights. The day grew darker. More luggage and packages loaded onto the bus and the exchange of conversation between the bus driver, bus station staff and the boarding passengers. Aluminum milk cans were loaded onto the bus.

The weather was frigid, and the bus windows were frosted over. Christmas lights in house windows and yards seen through the haze of frost. There were troubles and extra duties at every town for the driver. It was a sleepy day although sleep was never quite possible. Looking out the bus window the fields were covered white, the trees dusted half-white. Over the next few hours the snow storm did not subside. The light of day grew even grayer. In the small towns where we stopped all seemed quiet except for the arrival of the bus and the exiting and boarding of ticket holders. There was sudden activity, the sound of the luggage door on the side of the bus, looking out from the bus a view of people happy to see each other. Then we we're off to the next town. Signs advertised restaurants, antiques or a necessity of some sort many of these places of business dressed in strings of Christmas lights. It was Christmas time despite it all.

Some towns we passed through seemed lonelier perhaps because of a lack of activity. The Victorian houses we passed looked empty and rich in the snow. The snow still falling and travel across the roads slower. But the bus kept a cautious steady speed. At one point as we were leaving a town the wind seemed to grow even stronger and the blowing snow made visibility on the highway much worse. The lights of commercial stores along the route looked blurred. Cars used their windshield wipers. The headlights of passing cars and the street lights showed the fierce wind-blown snow. It was now early evening and outside my bus window the woods in the distance beyond the snow-covered fields were dark and barely visible. Slowly we made it home. Waterloo finally came into view, first the *Crossroads Center* shopping mall. *Sears* had added a triangle Christmas tree in green lights to their red-lettered logo, then past the residential streets with white wood houses with scattered yard decorations. Most of the light of day had faded and the city looked gray and winter-like. It was home and there was downtown, the buildings looking small and empty.

Christmas Writings

The Dime Store

We walked into the dime store downtown to look for necessities. It was close to Christmas and the free-standing merchandise bins and shelves were filled with decorations, toys and gift ideas, shiny ball ornaments, blue, green and gold, standard light sets, bubble lights or twinkle lights. Some were plugged in for our consideration. For sale were boxed Christmas cards with poinsettia or glitter snowy country scenes with sleds. There were chocolate-covered cherries, perfume sets, aftershave and plastic toys. Tubes of Christmas wrapping waited to be selected, Santa and Christmas bells, red and green plaid. Red and green tinsel garland decorated the camera counter. It was gray outside and snowing lightly. Christmas lights in the drug store across the street blinked on and off.

It was Christmas day and I was walking in the field behind my father's house. The wooded area that edged this field was on lower ground that the side street that ran alongside it. The Christmas lights that decorated the houses could be seen through the branches of the trees. It was almost too windy and cold to be outdoors. As I walked about I had thoughts of childhood Christmas memories.

At grade-school, I had made a paper and glitter ornament in the shape of a fabricated Moravian star. It decorated our tree that year. I remembered the construction-paper chains that decorated our thin spruce tree in our classroom. Christmas light bulbs were added, those large UL orange, green, blue and red bulbs that glowed brightly in the darkened hallway or fluorescent-lit classroom. I sang in the choir at church and school, an evening performance of Christmas music. A tour of the town's Christmas lights always included a drive down Prospect Boulevard with its grand houses set back on acres of lawn, all blue or green lights on coned-shaped ever-greens. Red lights outlined a large, white colonial door-entrance into a colonial brick mansion.

The wind grew stronger and the particles of snow swirled around me. The field was completely covered in snow except for the few remnants of brown weeds that edged the trees at its edge. The sight of it mixed with the thought of Christmas wrapping paper of opened gifts. Christmas day was cinnamon and cookies, peppermint candy canes and a Christmas dinner of ham or roast. How American is that. The neighborhood seemed quiet. People stayed indoors.

Christmas in Missouri

We spent Christmas at my Grandmother Bland's farm that year. I was a young boy and had received *The Jetson's* board game and clothes. I liked the cartoon *Jetson's* and their futuristic gadgets, and I liked the *Flintstones* as well, when the animation showed a sky of

124

stars above the stone houses and pre-historic palm trees. Snow covered the Missouri fields and woods that surrounded the farm. The linoleum floor cold in the mornings before the wood stove was re-started and stoked. Christmas seemed older, simpler, and more old-fashioned that year.

A Description of a Christmas in Iowa

It was a Christmas in a year I do not remember exactly. The winter was snowy, too gray and full of snow precipitation. The Christmas lights on houses and stores glowed in the frigid weather.

The mall had put up its flocked trees and giant candy canes. Christmas lights decorated the different departments at *Sears*, -Appliances, -Hardware and fake evergreen garland and red velvet ribbon trimmed the clothing displays. The corn fields near the mall and surrounding stores now stubble of corn stalks covered in snow.

Christmas performances were scheduled, Messiahs, church carolers. An Iowa college choir sang carols on television. Local TV stations dressed their logos in Santa caps and holly.

Relatives from Des Moines were traveling up to visit and an aunt would stop by with food and news of other relatives who lived long distances away. A bright red poinsettia plant occupied the center of our dining room table.

We had put up our decorations as well. Some old or new and store bought, some stenciled with glitter rings, frosted or shiny. The tree lost needles and the package under the tree that was department-store wrapped had a nice flat bow and foil paper. The wind outside shook the gray branches of trees. Exhaust from cars passing slowly rose steam-like. Snow crunched under our feet. The winter night sky a deep blue with a few low stars. The spot-lit nativity scene in front of a church looks lovely and sincere as we drive by at night. The words Peace On Earth are displayed in another church yard.

The Christmas Field

Christmas day is not a day to venture far. I mean from the house or the house of a relative-or wherever you might call home. My home was my father's house in Iowa. Attached to the field behind our house now mostly covered in snow and where I had ventured to one late afternoon day of Christmas many years back. That field was the ending of a place, the edge of our neighborhood, where streets ended and the last houses at its edge now had colorful UL Christmas bulbs outlining their windows and doors. Dad had made candles from melting wax and whipping it in a mixer to my mother's horror. The wax then mixed with food coloring and poured into a milk carton mold with a wick. The finished product sprinkled with glitter. One now glowed nicely on our TV set in the living room but was fading to a hollow failure. There was eggnog, too many cookies but not enough. Remembering the fact that the holiday was a religious celebration-looking up-the weather overcast gray sky, cold and flurries, a typical Iowa Christmas day.

Rudolph the Red Nose Reindeer is on television. There's a *Norelco* commercial on right now. I had wrapped two gifts just before the show started. The packages are now under the tree. The glowing Christmas lights on the tree reflect off the package's wrapping, green and blue and red. Rudolph has started and Burl Ives as a snowman is starting to sing his first song.

It was Christmas Eve and we took a tour of the Christmas lights in Waterloo. This was mostly through the upscale area of town. An area of grand, older homes on big lawns. The evergreen shrubs that framed the windows were lit in blue or green lights. Inside and through a picture window was a large, matching tree. Or gold or red lights hung from the trees in the yards. A green wreath on the door with a red ribbon. The larger yards with houses set back a distance from the boulevard had a Santa with reindeer or a nativity scene. Mechanical chiming Christmas bells rang on another house. Often at Christmas, we had snow and so the lights reflected on the snow-covered yards casting their light. Orange candles might have been placed on window sills seen as we listened to the slow crunching sound of snow beneath our car's tires. Then it was home where we watched a college choir sing carols on a local TV station. Mom wrapped one more gift and then we were all off to bed. It was another Christmas in Iowa.

Christmas 1970s

It was a week or so before Christmas. I was in my first year of high school. Snow covered the farm land that surrounded my Northeastern Iowa hometown. I now sat at my blue-painted desk in my attic room and I thought of what I had purchased at the shopping mall as Christmas gifts. These were a knit hat and scarf for my girlfriend, a shirt for my dad (that my mom had bought), a nice white blouse for my mom, a pair of gloves for my brother Vince and perfume and lotion sets for my sisters. I looked out the attic window that faced West and looked out towards our neighbor's front yard. Large outdoor blue, green and red Christmas bulbs decorated one of their tall evergreen trees in front of their flat-roofed house. Another neighbor had arrived home, their car slowly entering their concrete driveway. The snow was neatly shoveled to its edge. Exhaust drifted up from the car's tailpipe that evaporated into the frigid air. The cars red tail lights burned brighter before going dark. I could hear my mother's voice downstairs as she talked with my father. It had something to do with the holiday and an aunt and uncle. Then they talked about something needed to be purchased. A short argument ensued that my mother seemed to win easily. Our Christmas tree had long needles that year. It was wider but shorter. It had a new set of red, poinsettia-shaped Christmas bulbs on it. These along with our older collection of Christmas ornaments handed down by an aunt or from many years past when we children were very young. The piano along with its kerosene lamps had been decorated with a string of

128

Christmas twinkle lights, a nativity of painted clay characters, two wax-candle carolers and a ceramic-bell angel in a pretty red coat. I looked out the window for a time. Evening came slowly. The gray winter day of December began to turn to night. The street lights on Summit Street shown down on the snow and made shadows across the yards of the houses. In the distance down the street a few of the yard trees and front windows of the houses were lit up with Christmas lights. It was time for dinner. My mother was calling my name.

As Christmas approached things seemed quieter in the house although there was more activity. There was food to be made such as Christmas desserts and ingredients bought for a special casserole. It had stopped snowing outdoors and the snow lay silent on the ground with a crust of ice covering it. The tree branches were edged with ice and snow that clung to them despite gusts of snowy wind. Winter in Iowa was always white and gray-brown landscape against a gray sky. Lights glowed indoors, even the ordinary incandescent lights, as they now competed with Christmas lights on a tree and an occasional Christmas candle.

It is Christmas Eve and we are off to church. My mother is to sing a Christmas song, *O Holy Night*. It is snowing, but only lightly and it is very cold even for a December evening in Iowa. As my father drives us to church we pass two-story wood houses lit up with

Christmas lights around their windows or glowing red-chiming electric bells on a door. The lights on the Christmas trees seen indoors are dim by the indoor lighting of the house. The town seems quiet, Christmas Eve in on a Sunday evening this year. We are dressed in our Sunday clothes and my sister is wearing her new dress with a green velvet bodice. My mother is wearing here Christmas wreath pin on her coat. The lights of the church are dimmer this evening and red poinsettia plants line the church alter. My mother sings her song, a bit nervously, but her voice is lovely and it is mother's voice. There is a quiet after she sings. Christmas is a celebration. It is red and green and the smell of evergreen boughs. It is wrapping paper in rolls yet unused. It is tinsel from Christmas past.

Chapter 20

It was a quiet Sunday at church. Congregants were away on summer vacations. My visit home announced by our preacher the most important church news of the day.

The heat rendered the day silent; the summer sound of crickets louder than the daily noise of humans. It was a day to drift in thought.

On the way home, we stopped at the local *Hy-Vee*. Watermelons and cantaloupes were on sale, a fourth of July display of streamers and American flags decorated the produce.

Near the college, at the shopping center mall, a new kitchen-wares store had opened and was selling gleaming espresso machines and fancy kitchen gadgets.

Summer evenings in Iowa had always been sliced tomatoes from the garden, chocolate ice-cream, gnats and humidity, frying chicken and boiling corn on the kitchen stove, clutter and noise, sparse daily news and then finally a cool evening breeze and the quiet of night.

You return home again. You're now older. The place seems abandoned. Where are all those teenagers? And the church congregation much smaller, so small in fact, you wondered what happened? Of course, the downtown stores empty. Places you returned to -but it had all pretty much remained the same -probably.

No one knows you are home except family. It might be summer. People had simply moved on. Places change -close.

We drove North up through scenic *Devil's Backbone State Park*, past the farms and cornfields of Iowa arriving in Decatur just past noon. The river flowed through town. Efforts to preserve the town's more historic buildings made the place look like a movie-set. It was a lovely, quiet Iowa town but it suddenly seemed odd to me that we would lose our mother to cancer soon and this place would remain the same. She asked for a *Pepsi-Cola* with lunch and we pretended that she wasn't sick, but the grief was silent in our hearts. It was a touching scene. The small-town restaurant's lunch counter, the young, high school girl who waited on us, the others in the restaurant just simple, Iowa folk. Another look at the river, time enough to enjoy the sunshine, the fresh air and we headed back for home.

On the way, back my parents conversed in the car. How odd it seemed that they were pointing out nice houses along the way to own. Never giving up the thought, the two of them casual in their conversation, both knowing my mother would not live much longer.

That summer my dad mowed lawns and sold cattails to the local grocery stores. Sold at places like the new mall-area *Hy-Vee* in the floral department. He kept going, made himself useful. My mother grew sicker. It was dreadful.

In November, when she was finally gone it didn't seem real at first, as death never does I suppose, not really. We felt the grief but the person remained in silence, in the embrace of a neighbor who brought you food and hugged you. A neighbor you didn't really know.

My mother had spent much of her life connected to our Methodist church. Teaching Sunday school; helping with weddings, showers missionary related events. In the social area room where the old sanctuary with stain-glass windows and wood pews darkly varnished. The thud sound of a hymnal being put away, the friendly whisper of a congregant or the preacher, then a voice, a command and the sound of the piano, the old-fashioned, gospel hymns sung were different but the same, by congregants grown old or somehow taken from us and gone to heaven.

It remained cold that winter. The weather was frigid, so below-zero cold you would never fully remember it. It seemed to make the mornings quieter, the gray overcast days longer. The world had become inhabitable. The only visible movement outside was the smoke from the house's chimneys. And there was the sound of crunching snow.

Our family dinner table set. The six o'clock news. My mother's voice. My father's response. The corner grocery, *Buzzby Wing Drugstore*, our church, a school function held in the fluorescent light of a weekday evening. That was and is Iowa to me.

Chapter 21

_____

October 31, 2001

It was Halloween day and late afternoon when I first looked up at the sky. I saw a sky like gray marble with a bright sliver of light along the horizon revealing a glimpse of the world's edge. It was October thirty-first and it was said that there was to be a Halloween full moon this year, that very evening. I had read this in the newspaper. This had not occurred for almost a half century. And too, the seven-star constellation would be at its highest point in the sky, which according to myth would occur during a great calamity! The Aztecs and Mayans believed it would be overhead at midnight on the night the world comes to an end. I thought of the pumpkin patch that someone had planted years ago near our house on Summit Street just at the edge of *Black Hawk Creek*, an arching sort of patch of land that seemed mysterious at its edge -now long gone. I was staying at my father's cabin near the Cedar River a distance from the lights of town and that Halloween night I saw a perfect full moon through the gnarly tree branches of an Oak surrounded by drifting gray clouds and one that resembled a witch on a broom! This was that very dreaded full moon predicted so many years ago!

Who could forget past Halloweens? Was anything on television like *Charlie Brown's, The Great Pumpkin*? This was before the DVD. The light in the living room seemed more dramatic for some reason. The candle in the jack-o-lantern is crackling and flickering too much. There are bowls of candy on the table in the hall near the front door.

It is Halloween night. I am twelve years old and although I am almost too old to go trick-or-treating, I go anyway to get one last year's bag of candy. I cover every block as far as the elementary school. I venture into the nicer neighborhood around Home Park Boulevard. The evening has grown darker and I am growing tired. I check inside the bag. *Reese's Peanut Butter Cups*, tiny bars of *Hershey* chocolate; *Milky Way*, bags of candy corn, caramel candy, more chocolate bars; *Snickers*. I return home. Our pumpkin is still lit but has shriveled a bit. It smells of charred pumpkin. Tomorrow is a school day.

I loved the changing seasons in Iowa. The chilly edge of fall or walking on a cold winter afternoon. A perfect, breezy spring day or July in Iowa that was usually too hot and humid.

By the early 1980s, Waterloo, Iowa had changed. The Danish-modern breakfront in the dining room area of our house didn't match the new colonial-American table and dining room chairs my parents had bought. The light fixture in this dining room was new as well. Also, a colonial style with burnt-orange glass. It reflected their changing tastes.

Our neighborhood had changed in ways. Added onto, run down and built up. The field behind our house was now a girls' softball diamond with bleachers. Old Mrs. Janson and her funny brown-shingled house was only a distant memory. The high school prom tuxedo was still in the window of the formal wear shop downtown, but it was now a pastel blue with a cool ruffled shirt. The eighties brought AIDS. Things being the way they were, it was a matter of survival. I went home for visits almost annually. I coveted the old wood houses, particularly the ones with some architectural interest. The solitude they offered, in this small town of no real importance except that it was home. You never really recover the past. It is impossible, only the edge of it. But the memories shade the same places. It's an odd mix -really, of typically middle-American memories. The simplest things remembered, now seem magnified and then you realize how important children are. What their life experience means. The color of something, the change of a shadow to light, light itself, daylight, incandescent, the fluorescent-lit hallway of a school building at night, a silence before bedtime and the dark of night. You discovered things like *Kon Tiki* glassware hidden away. You remember the shellacking on the kitchen cabinets, spray starch, garden tomatoes, the smell of freshly ironed linens to be put away in the linen closet as told and the fluffy topping on lemon-meringue pie.

It was a winter morning. I was riding the Waterloo city bus. Across the snow-covered fields and along the horizon the rising sun looked like a giant tangerine of liquid mercury behind the web of black tree branches and evergreen shapes. I thought of my winters in

Iowa while growing up. There were frigid winter days when the snow was covered with a crusty ice.

It was now May 17, my mother's birthday. It was a familiar rain and a wind only as distant as the trees outside my window. I had stood at an open window in the kitchen smelling the soggy earth. This was a fresh morning rain and with it came chunks of hail that crackled and bounced against the green roof shingles and windowpanes of the house. I thought of my mother and I going to the *Ben Franklin* store on Kimball Avenue when I was a teenager. There were greeting cards and nice stationary you only bought to give to someone else. Those greeting cards would later be found in a desk drawer or in heaps of papers in cardboard box, like small records of a time, symbolizing expressed love and the passing of time.

The seasons of the year were expressed in church as well. As part of a sermon. The clothes we wore changed. Warm coats and boots put on in winter. New clothes for Easter. A short-sleeve shirt or lighter-weight cotton dress worn to a Wednesday night, summer church meeting. We heard about children that had moved away. People that had died or about a planned baby shower, wedding or camp-grounds meeting somewhere in a small-town North of Waterloo. All these events important to us, or at least they seemed as such in an after-church service conversation. We usually went home for dinner or we might go out to the *Crossroads Mall Bishops* for a meal. If it were a birthday or we had relatives staying with us that weekend.

What did *Bishops* offer to eat? Porcelain dish servings of cold slaw, lettuce and tomato mini-salads, fish in a white sauce or meatloaf with gravy. Side orders of green beans or butter beans. Desserts like chocolate pie with chocolate shavings or just a square serving of *Jello*. You could have a roll or slices of bread with butter. Then off with your tray to a dining room that had a brick fireplace, wallcovering and color-matching carpet.

Chapter 22

When writing this book, I tried to remember specific events. Most events seemed ordinary but this one afternoon has always stayed with me as if it were yesterday.

There was a small, gray-shingled house that occupied a small yard on a dead-end street that was just West of the field behind our house. This belonged to the widow, Mrs. Barker. This house is now long gone. My mother did Mrs. Barker's permanent for her, this tight henna-colored pin curls all wet and bobby-pinned. This old lady, Mrs. Barker would sit in one of our dining-room chairs with her orthopedic shoes on, her legs leisurely extended and crossed, chatting it up with mom.

One Saturday afternoon I walked with my mother over to Mrs. Barker's house. It was a cute house that really belonged to the rural past of this area. Mom had asked me to come along and bring paper sacks for apples. Mrs. Barker had offered to give us as many as we wanted. I gathered the apples that had fallen onto the ground as there were many, and I began to fill the grocery sacks that I had brought.

"I'll make several apple cobblers with those," my mother said.

We left Mrs. Barker a bag of apples as well. She still "baked some too" and would need the tree apples for canning. I carried the apples home under a charcoal-gray sky and the sprinkling of rain. The summer sky had suddenly darkened as if almost night. How quickly it had changed. The weather was only warm. There was an eerie silence and then the Waterloo city tornado sirens went off. Then a terrible thunderstorm broke. After the tornado watch was lifted we drove to *Eagle* grocery to get cinnamon, sugar and baking products. It was one of the few times I was truly frightened by the weather and I listened to the weather report on the car's radio as mom drove us to *Eagle*s. We lived through it and had apple cobbler that night.

It is early fall again in Iowa. At the *National Dairy Cattle Congress*, we saw all sorts of people. People from Iowa mostly. Some obviously living on farms as they were tending to animals. Crowds of people that had walked from their cars and were now in line to see the fair. There were still errands to run that day. The practicality of life. We noticed the nicer homes and yards we passed on our way home. We soon forgot about our plastic bag of souvenirs; mostly brochures, balloons and items like calendars, car window scrapers, etc.

Chapter 23

The area around *Black Hawk Creek* was located directly behind the field that edged our backyard area and was named *Injun Country* and was part of *Hope C. Martin Park*. This *Injun Country* Park was created during the nineteen sixties. There is a photograph of our family standing next to the *Injun Country* sign as if on a holiday, my dad and us children in shorts. I think mom took the photograph. It must be a summer day as the sunlight in the photographs seems bright. An iconic family photograph that reminds me of the picnics we had during the summer months. I also remember one church youth group outing when we attempted to swim in this muddy creek. I remember the warm creek water, the oozing mud beneath my feet, floating weeds and the gnats and bugs that flew about above the water's surface. I preferred *Byrnes Park* swimming pool. *Injun Country* park had historic information signpost along new paths, metal Tipis, totem poles. A wood fort made of logs and a camping area.

This was the camp site of the Pottowattomie, Fox, Sioux, Winnebago and Sac Indians. This was also a camp site for the pioneers who camped on the far side of *Black Hawk Creek*. (CardCow.com, postcard image, Injun Country, Hope C. Martin Park)

This park seemed to suit the time, the 1960s and early 1970s. I remember going into one of the aluminum tipis. It was fun and silly. The thing made a hollow sound. There was a place for campers to stay overnight with electrical outlets for the campers. All of this is gone now. I have searched for information on the area and had great difficulty finding any specific information outside of the fact that the area was once inhabited by the Fox and Sauk Indians. It made me look closer at the land, the geographical place, the older trees, granite stones, creek areas that have remained the same.

Due to the annual flooding in this area of Waterloo, banks of earth have been built up alongside *Black Hawk Creek*, as part of the urban renewal projects of Waterloo. The flood control movement. This park area, *Hope C. Martin Park*, had a trail along the creek with aluminum tipis and signposts that told the area's history. Much of this land area has been taken up by a new highway but what little remains is still a place of simple beauty. There are many old trees, many of these trees oak and there are still older specimens of elm despite the Dutch elm disease that destroyed many of this once common species native to Iowa during the past century. Large patches of wild violets and dandelions grow thick beneath the trees. Oak, maple and elm leaves collect on the ground during the fall months and violets persist until the first snowfall.

This creek land area, to me as a boy was a place of magic, a place where the spirit of the Indians lived-on. The Indian dwellings are still visible in the wigwam-hive shapes of twigs and dried grass that have formed in the sedge grass along the riverbank.

Open ground areas are covered with fallen branches and broken twigs. There are areas of land where the sunlight reflects a change of color in the grass or in the thick leaves and wild violets that cover the ground surrounding the trees. The tree bark seems darker and the landscape colors somehow change with occurrence; the passing of time and the chance reflection of the morning sun. Closer to a more wooded area there is a place covered with large granite stones. A crow caws. A mockingbird's sudden flight flashes wings of white and black feathers.

I remember a place near the creek's edge with hanging vines and shadows. It is closer to summer now and the purple of violets is scarcer under the trees. There are bugs visible in the air and on the creek's surface.

Chapter 24

———————

It was that last trip home from New York City. I arrived on the Greyhound bus. Maxine from our church had met me at the bus station looking so nice in her ruby-red suit. I was given a key to my father's summer cabin in Cedar Falls. My hometown of Waterloo, Iowa seemed so quiet; wonderfully small and quiet. The Cedar River flowing lazy that day, the October sun hidden behind a thin haze of cloud. Who would leave this place, so safe and simple and adequate? Much of the town was the same. The big wood houses on shady, peaceful streets.

Returning here on a bus, the town doesn't exist at all until you reach its very edge. I have never seen land so flat and parceled as Iowa land; acres of assigned corn and grazing fields with radio towers and telephone lines marking every inch. Then you're there, home and you see a few trees and houses and then the *Crossroads Shopping Mall* comes into view. Somehow it becomes three-dimensional again and the land is varied too in places but only slightly. You see familiar names and business and then you're getting off the bus.

There's a history to the place not completely erased and you look for the clues to this past. At least I did because it was where I grew up. It's new and practical and never quite neglected as you might hope it is at times. Leave it the same you might say to yourself.

There had been visits home to Waterloo, Iowa during the winter. You remembered small things like the crunching sound of snow beneath your feet or the lonely shadows cast on the buildings downtown as you walked to a parked car. Changes like a new gas station or convenience store, aluminum-sided and glowing in fluorescent greenish light.

Over the years I returned many times on the bus. The following is a recent memory.

How small and modest your hometown looks, returning on a cold winter's day on the bus from Chicago, all gray and cold; aluminum siding. The bushes along the two-story wood houses covered with clumps of snow.

A neon sign advertising a bakery, OPEN. It is a newly-built structure that almost resembled a house. There are new convenience stores with displays of bananas and cafe mocha ready to be served into paper cups stacked neatly next to the coffee machine. The mall area slowly growing alongside the adjacent cornfields.

I had visited many times over the years and I had enjoyed these visits. Waterloo always seemed such a livable place. The surrounding rural areas around Waterloo, farther out towards its edges are half-field and half farms. Some of the land is cornfield. Tall grass grows along fences and gravel roadsides. The weather is hot and sticky with humid during the summers. The winters bring snowdrifts and chilling wind.

Chapter 25

_____

I remember one school day when my older brother and sister and I remained at school during a lunch hour for lunch. My mother had an appointment that day and so she had packed us a paper bag lunch of lunch-meat and white-bread sandwiches (with lots of mayonnaise) in waxed paper and cookies.

My older brother always seemed to be the center of abuse for some reason at school and this lunchtime was no different. All I remember was that the teacher who monitored this classroom where we ate was asking my brother what the first day of the week was on a calendar. She now held the calendar in her hand. My brother paused, thought then replied, Monday. This was of course wrong, -it was Sunday and the teacher corrected my brother with unusual scorn. We finished our lunch in silence, but I remember thinking that there was a message or lesson outside of that correct answer, Sunday.

I walk past the red brick school house where I attended grade school. There is the smell of paste glue on construction paper. The kind that sticks to your fingers and must be washed off in the low porcelain sink. Milk glass light fixtures hang from the ceiling of the school room and Van Gogh's *Starry Night* floats above the neatly printed Alphabet above the black board. There is a drinking fountain in the hallway with cold water to drink. The walls are shiny in the dim light and the sound of footsteps echo off its walls.

I passed by this grade school, named *Whittier Elementary School*, many times while living in Waterloo. It was gutted now and the windows had been removed. They had begun renovating the old brick, two-story building to make residential housing units. Bits of plaster and red-clay bricks lay in the schoolyard of the school building. Bits of wall plaster painted primary colors of pale green and yellow. Voices from the past echoed off school walls.

Tossed out a school room window was plaster painted lime green, bright yellow and glossy. Chalky sections of wall plaster with paint peeling in places. It brought me back to our elementary school *Weekly Readers* and brown-bag lunches of egg salad sandwiches. A horrible, chalk blackboard *squeak* and rainy morning cloakroom raincoats.

From *Whittier School*, I walked the short distance of a few blocks to the street where my parent's house still stood. How long a walk it had seemed when I was a child. Winter snow storms, icicles and giant snowdrifts came to mind. I thought of the retired Quaker minister we knew that lived in a white wood house with an oval-shaped window. The new owners of our house on Summit Street had added onto the house, a much larger addition that had most probably increased the value of the house a good deal. I walked out to the field behind our house still accessible. It was now city land and a girl's baseball diamond, but the edge of the property was still wooded, and weeds and clover grew near the trees. There was a day, one day, when the sun covered by clouds re-appeared to shine. And it did now as a memory of that day, patches of ice covering the leaves and weeds. I notice the colors, yellow and mauve, varied greens-most of it weeds but still as beautiful as I remember.

It was the very last of summer and an Indian summer day. The grass in the field was thick and dried brown and gnats and bugs filled the air. There was clover in the grass. The field quiet and motionless in the late-summer daylight with patches of clear blue sky between scarce clouds half-hiding the sun. This field was once filled with tall weeds and sedge grass, brown dried ragged weeds, pods, others green flowering yellow and mauve. Butterflies, gnats, bee and bugs filled the air. Summer was hot and burning, the sky intense blue with scattered clouds. Then there was the sudden color of fall. The trees knew more than we did about the calendar and soon the days were cooler and nightfall came earlier than we had expected. Violets still under the trees would soon be hidden by leaves. The leaves then covered with the first snow of winter.

Only the very edges of this field remain and a narrow section of trees, the Manning's wonderful garden was gone. The land where apple trees stood and the arching pumpkin patch paved over by the new highway.

After walking outside on a day, perhaps a late afternoon or early evening, having walked to nowhere really, just away from the house to the field nearby, to the trees that edged this field on a day suddenly cold, perhaps the beginning of fall or even winter and then indoors. Here it was the same and would be for an indeterminate period for there was still time to love, to share or to be angry at, but looking back on those days anger seems a waste of time and the opportunity to express love to those now gone-well what we wouldn't give for that-after walking outside on a day-any day.

I had reached the corner grocery now an auto-part store and kept on walking. The tree shaded boulevards in this small town on a spring or summer day are wonderful. Usually peaceful and quiet. Manicured lawns or un-mowed grass in a backyard. A garden of flowers and tomato plants. Children were playing.

Chapter 26

It was January, gray and filled with the sound of wind. Snow clinging to the rough bark of trees. Gardens covered in snow drifts. The dark windows of houses edged with frost. It was the beginning of a new year. In a few short months, spring would come green and budding. This if we kept trudging through the snow on a narrow path scraped by snow shovels.

It was during a January snowstorm, a real snowstorm this time, a genuine blizzard. Channel Seven News had declared it. But all the same it was a beautiful evening. It was unusually light for that time of evening and under the downtown street lights the closed storefronts of our Iowa town looked timeless in the great drifts of snow that now covered a good portion of their facades.

Near this area and on the edge of commercial downtown was a very beautiful, large old oak tree. That snowy, windy night the shadows of this tree's branches danced wildly against the sky. Its shadow cast onto an exposed brick wall of an adjacent building and onto the ground below it. It was a sight I shared with no one until now. It seemed to represent something of the past; endurance and strength of spirit. And I thought of the Cotton Wood tree near our house now gone.

There were many places in this town where I had a sense of the past. A yard with old trees, lots of shade, half-garden, attached to an old, wood house most probably built in the 1930s or 1940s. The two-story kind with a comfortable, screen-enclosed porch.

I thought of that tiny house nears ours. Up the street, up the hill from where I grew up. Its windows covered with plastic in the winter since it lacked proper storm windows. A tiny cement-block house with lily of the valley and iris growing alongside the house. The grass overgrown and unmoved. A broken, crooked sidewalk leading to its front door. Some old person must have lived there, leftover from the past. Inside, funny- patterned linoleum-covered floors. Houseplants crowded the windows. Furnishings sparse and rickety.

One very large house on the downtown, East side of town, a Victorian was slowly being renovated. It was the largest Victorian house I had ever seen and it was a joy to see its many bay windows and balconies being re-built. How long had it stood there abandoned? Who would bother with such a beautiful, expensive monstrosity?

And there were those boxy wood houses on stilts in that poorest part of town near the river that was flooded annually from the spring rains.

I found an apartment in Waterloo. It was a nice place with hardwood floors and an old-fashioned kitchen reminiscent of the nineteen forties. Lily of the valley grew in bunches alongside the apartment building. An Asian couple lived on the first floor of the building and their unlikely garden covered one narrow, neatly toiled, side-section of the yard. It was a wonderful leafy-green garden with

Chinese vegetables, cabbage and lettuce. Every inch of yard space available was used. It was a wonderful sight to see.

I did a lot of writing. I remember one rainy night while residing there in particular. The booming sound of thunder so loud it shook the building, great flashes of lightening. I stared out at a torrential, dark rain outside. One late afternoon the light of the warm day came through the window like a dancing vapor, fading to evening as I read a book.

The downtown public library held a used book sale in the basement of their building. Bright fluorescent lighting lit the basement aisles of the discarded titles one Saturday morning. There were a few finds, books by James Michner, Pearl Buck and F. Scott Fitzgerald.

And why was I writing? I had little choice really, a writer writes; destined to I suppose. A constant struggle to stay employed had left me with too much time to waste and I found myself writing one day in a tablet.

I remember one summer day in Waterloo, Iowa while living in this apartment. It was the same summer day we all experience in our lives, and not from any singular year. For me that day was humidity. It was the sound of yard crickets. A day as fixed as the box fan in my apartment that helped bring in an outdoor breeze from an open window.

I wanted to make copies of some writings to send out to a publisher, so I headed downtown nearby to a storefront printing &

copy and paper store that occupied one of the old red-brick buildings. That day the town street looked to me like an Edward Hopper or Charles E. Burchfield painting, in that it was so typical in its small-town, American perspective. The printer-copy store's door was open but another screen door, to keep out the dust and bugs, was kept closed. How this place stayed open I will never know for it was an almost empty storefront. The floor was concrete, and the ceiling was made of the same decorative, tin sheeting material you see in these old, often empty building storefronts. A single lamp on a metal desk illuminated the almost space. Sunlight from a front window provided the rest of the dim, diffuse light in the room. I got my copies and I headed for home. Outside it was quiet. Crab grass grew between the cracked sidewalks. It was near the railroad tracks.

Chapter 27

I looked for work and finally found employment, working for *Sears, Roebuck & Co.*, as a catalog sales employee. This position was through a company that had been contracted to hire individuals for this sort of work. After a couple of weeks of training, I donned a pair of headsets and began cheerfully taking phone orders from the *Sears* Catalogs. There were several now, one for bedding and home accessory items, one for outdoor and patio furniture, and another catalog for general merchandise including clothing. The customer was always right no matter how agitated and although I found the work difficult at times, I stuck it out on a full-time basis. This work lasted perhaps five months or so until the staff was cut as the orders had dwindled a bit. I left one rather odd, confrontational morning after stubbornly showing up for work despite a lack of it, as previously told by a disgruntled manager. I had lasted much longer than any of the others hired at the same time as I had been hired. The only remaining trainee except for a very small group of long-timers, a group of pleasant ladies that kept pretty much to themselves. Work in Waterloo was scarce and many of the jobs paid a minimum wage.

I continued to look for work everywhere. Each morning I dressed myself and headed out. Today it was the car sales lots, one was nearby where I lived. In fact, on the same lot where the old *Eagle's* grocery had been. Then I headed out to the new car sales lots near the shopping center. Sure, I had experience in sales and I confidently filled out the applications. I sat in the local day-labor employment office at 6am with countless other men eager for a day's wage. I was old enough to be their father and when asked if I was strong enough for a job that was pending I would say without hesitation, yes. I lifted weights at the gym. Yet, only twice was I sent out. Once to unload large sheets of plywood from a truck to a house in Cedar Falls. Four hours times eight dollars minus taxes, paid out immediately for a small fee from a machine at the agency. Another time, I helped clean an industrial company's garage and mowed their back lawn. They at first claimed that we had not put in our minimum four hours of work. The company refused to pay us because of this. One of the guys on the job was "just passing through town," not having found work in his Southern home state. We did get paid eventually for the four-hour minimum, but only after a long wait sitting outside in front of the company. After a few weeks of unsuccessful job searching, I was forced to leave my apartment. I had made a very good effort at finding work. I tried not to blame myself. Life had simply not brought me to the best place.

One afternoon when I was living in Waterloo I wandered into a used furniture store-thrift shop near where I lived. It was filled with junk really but there were a few nice, old pieces of furniture and items one might need like a bookshelf. On the walls hung a kitschy assortment of framed artwork, most of it tacky, supermarket cardboard prints of famous paintings. Or worse, like one abstract framed thing made of faded yarn. But one image captured my attention. It was a European print scene of Venice, Italy. Venice never looked so accessible.

I had orange sherbet and ice-cream bars at the *Dairy Queen* and an *A & W* root beer. I went to hear a summer band concert one evening at *Byrnes Park*. A concert of Broadway show tunes and patriotic anthems.

I endlessly haunted the antique stores downtown in search of the past and found art pottery, inkwells and old radios, even crispy paper bags and hatboxes from *Black's*.

I found the main floor of *Black's Department Store* building open, but it was now mostly empty. There was a small coffee and sandwich shop along one side of the window space that served the downtown businesses. In another window alcove, an antiques dealer sold odds and ends. I tried to imagine the place as it must have been in the 1920s. Its elegant two-storied main floor with glass cases displaying men's neckties and lady's accessories.

It's good to let go of the past and to move forward with things. It wasn't as great at it all seemed, but then it was at times. The people you loved were still living. Simple can be better, quality better than shoddy. The past was good in many ways.

If you looked for this town on a map of the U.S., you might not find it. It seemed more livable to me than other places but perhaps this is because it was home. There's a logic to it and what is not here, you might find in Chicago, Illinois.

Living in Waterloo for a time, I walked and I wandered and people in town must have noticed me from time to time.

"That fellow from New York," one rather unpleasant woman once called me one day and she was right really, for once a New Yorker always a New Yorker. But this Iowa town was home to me.

I can't say I like the flatness of the Iowa landscape, the sameness of the thousands of acres of corn and soy that cover the state but there are beautiful scenic places and magnificent prairie land where the Mormons crossed on their way to the promise land out West.

It is a summer day, pleasant and solitary. The smallness of this place makes you feel safe. Children play in the yards. It is the middle of nowhere, the Midwest; tranquil. The grocery store advertises local produce in their flyer. It all looks old-fashioned; baskets of cherries, cantaloupes, half-shucked ears of corn. Shop here and not at *Wal-Mart* or that new *Target* with a discount grocery.

I have experienced this place in all seasons; rainstorms and snowstorms, hot humid summer evenings and breezy spring days. In extreme seasons of frigid winter mornings with smoke billowing from silent sleeping houses when I rode with my father to work so my mother could have use of the car. In thunderstorms that could frighten me away from a window. On windy, fall days when leaves filled the air or during a hail storm that pelted the roof of our house noisily. It is why I returned to this place. To feel the summer heat

157

and winter cold. To see the wood houses and trees covered in snow. The fireflies and dandelions and violets thick in the yards of people I didn't know. How miraculous it all seemed when I was a child.

In Iowa, there is a garden. It is the kind of garden with blackberry bushes and flowers; annuals you wouldn't recognize because they were old-fashioned. It is the best kind of garden, slightly overgrown, and with rhubarb hiding under its own thick leaves, stalks of sour maroon with earth-roots whitish.

Chapter 28

Being different can set you apart, but it can also offer a wider perspective of things. It can be ironic and humorous to notice the obvious that others will not, or care not to notice. Human need often goes unnoticed and that can be your own. I am a great believer in hope. Forgiveness can be difficult. Having the patience to listen can be a start. You find that your story is not so unusual and part of someone else's your own. Home or a hometown is something you never reach, as a part of it is steeped in the past. Many people that were a part of my growing up had gone for one reason or another. But the weather remained, the changing seasons. The summer months were not as hot and humid as I remember but the rain was the same. A Midwest rain I can only describe as steady and comforting. Different neighbors had disrupted houses previously lived in by people I had known once. Old people or couples with children grown and moved away. I liked my walks home. It was a reason to pass the yards and houses, flowers and trees of years past. I noticed areas that did not seem recognizable. Places were gone or renovated. There were new additions, city projects that made space more practical.

And there were small fads that home owners copied from each other like new a new wood deck area and expanded steps leading to an older house, mostly unused.

The structures we build or add onto of course are very telling of us as a people. And much of what was seen spoke of peoples wish for privacy or stated the fact that they were not accessible for the most part. We don't use our deck. We're indoors and want to be left alone. Maybe they didn't care, or they were just too busy to use that front deck. It looked nice though and someday they would, some day or evening when the weather was nice. But it often made the houses look more vacant.

As I have grown older perhaps some of the magic of this place has faded in my thoughts. I am glad that I started those short stories many years back. Reading them reminds me of how important simple things are to a child. Like an encouragement or a holiday; the anticipation of a celebration, weddings and birthdays and moments of personal memory that we never express to anyone else not even in a book such as this. One morning while living there, I had a task that took me on a walk near the Cedar River downtown. The sight of this river in morning brought me back to when I lived here with my family. The times we drove across a downtown bridge on our way to a store or returning home after picking my father up from the meat packing plant.

Walking as much as I did in Waterloo, I saw much of it. I walked past the pizzeria that was once popular with high-school kids. The gardens and yards. The Presbyterian church with its hickory trees. There was that place that sold antiques on a highway near the bowling alley that was there when I was a child. They sold matching salt and pepper shakers, crocks, collectibles and a whole assortment of stuff. Past our Wesleyan church and attached parsonage. Past the house of the two girls I went to school with who liked to sew and wore fringed blouses and other homemade threads.

I imagine the empty downtown storefronts again filled with past tenants. The fabrics store. The ladies dress shop and the place that sold appliances and sewing machines. There, just as that one winter night when you were with a parent or a sibling for whatever reason now driving home. But first to the grocery store, then home to put away the carton of milk and loaf of bread. It is early but late; almost seven o'clock.

Iowa is crab grass around a vegetable garden with a few flowers; zinnias and bees. Homegrown tomatoes, blue-glass, *Mason* jars sitting empty on a shelf. The four seasons complete and often harsh.

It is an evening from long ago. The dinner dishes are done, and outside the early evening sky has turned from dark-blue to gray. Then the rain comes, in splashes at first, onto the grass and hard dusty earth that absorbs it quickly. My father already sleeping after a hard day's work at the packing plant. My mother reading a book from the library in a chair next to a table lamp. I look out a window of the house wondering if anyone else has noticed the night sky with its lightning and thunder. The rain falls harder now and the leaves of the trees, still visible, dance in the falling rain drops. Then the evening fades to night.

It is fall, perhaps a day in late October. It was sunny and warmer during the afternoon, but now towards early evening, it has suddenly turned very cold. A strong wind blows the leaves of the trees and stirs the leaves on the ground into drifting heaps. Our supper will consist of fried chicken and mashed potatoes and an opened can of green beans. There is left over spice-cake with a butterscotch frosting in the refrigerator that we will have for dessert. We will attend church service on Sunday morning and perhaps on a Sunday evening as well. The new green velvet sofa in our living room space with a floral pattern doesn't match the room's carpet but it still looks nice. A colonial-style glass lamp with a shade sits on an oval end table that also is of a colonial style. Near this table rests library books and our bible. I go outdoors for a moment and walk around barefoot. I notice the weather, the force of the wind, as if no one else notices. My dad will rise early at 5 am for a day at the packing plant. He will lose this job in the next few years when the meatpacking plant closes, this after I leave for college. But for now, he is employed and is going to bed early as he usually does.

While living in Waterloo as an adult, I remember one warm, sunny day walking in downtown Waterloo. It was a day of stillness and shadows. The streets seemed empty of humanity, having left along with the past. Yet, I remained to observe and to write about a place from another era. An America more tied to conversation and activity, that involved actual physical interaction and opinions of a more personal and regional kind. In my action of returning home, I too had let go of the past, but I also wanted to document it in this book, because I recognized a loss in the passing of it. A lost grace and an opportunity for philosophical union. In an unspoken dialogue of the senses. The underlying theme here is the value of interpersonal human interaction within society. That still happens, but less so as we become attached to communication-age technology and social media. Without that immediate access to computers and cell phones, we were slower in our responses and reflected of them on a more private level. Until the choice of sharing those responses, our opinions and ideas, seemed appropriate and necessary. This was an expression of our unique selves, physically present and revealed. It reminds me of those dinner table conversations that we had with family friends and relatives, often attached to photo albums and food.

October 2015

This was my first visit home during a fall month in many years.

My father resides at a nursing home. I went to visit my sister and we drove around our old neighborhood and past our house on Summit Street. There was the mood that autumn brought to this place. The sky was blue. The trees marking the fall season with orange, yellow and red leaves falling to the ground. That typical fall day, the wind caused the dried leaves on the ground to drift. But this time, I was not walking home while swooshing through the fallen leaves with my feet.

It wasn't until I had almost completed this book that I realized something about my mother. Those times when I was very young and she held my hand out of fear, saying she was afraid when we crossed the bridge, or walked around downtown. It wasn't out of fear for her, but for me. Like all children, I was simply too important to lose.

Not to fear! We've made it across the bridge.

The End

Printed in the United States

166

CPSIA information can be obtained
at www.ICGtesting.com
Printed in the USA
BVHW042144271218
536578BV00006B/79/P